The Future of Society

Blackwell Manifestos

In this new series major critics make timely interventions to address important concepts and subjects, including topics as diverse as, for example: Culture, Race, Religion, History, Society, Geography, Literature, Literary Theory, Shakespeare, Cinema, and Modernism. Written accessibly and with verve and spirit, these books follow no uniform prescription but set out to engage and challenge the broadest range of readers, from undergraduates to postgraduates, university teachers and general readers – all those, in short, interested in ongoing debates and controversies in the humanities and social sciences.

Already Published

The Idea of Culture   Terry Eagleton
The Future of Christianity   Alister E. McGrath
Reading After Theory   Valentine Cunningham
21st-Century Modernism   Marjorie Perloff
The Future of Theory   Jean-Michel Rabaté
True Religion   Graham Ward
Inventing Popular Culture   John Storey
The Idea of Latin America   Walter D. Mignolo
Myths for the Masses   Hanno Hardt
The Rhetoric of Rhetoric   Wayne C. Booth
The Future of War   Christopher Coker
When Faiths Collide   Martin E. Marty
The Idea of English Ethnicity   Robert Young
The Future of Environmental Criticism   Lawrence Buell
The Future of Society   William Outhwaite

Forthcoming

What Cinema Is!   Dudley Andrew
The Battle for American Culture   Michael Cowan
The Idea of Evil   Peter K. Dews
Television: Literate at Last   John Hartley
The Idea of Economy   Deirdre McCloskey

The Future of Society

William Outhwaite

Blackwell
Publishing

BLACKWELL PUBLISHING

350 Main Street, Malden, MA 02148-5020, USA
9600 Garsington Road, Oxford OX4 2DQ, UK
550 Swanston Street, Carlton, Victoria 3053, Australia

First published 2006 by Blackwell Publishing Ltd

1 2006

Library of Congress Cataloging-in-Publication Data

The future of society / by William Outhwaite.
p. cm. — (Blackwell manifestos)
Includes bibliographical references and index.
ISBN-13: 978-0-631-23185-1 (hardback : alk. paper)
ISBN-10: 0-631-23185-4 (hardback : alk. paper)
ISBN-13: 978-0-631-23186-8 (pbk. : alk. paper)
ISBN-10: 0-631-23186-2 (pbk. : alk. paper)
1. Postmodernism—Social aspects. 2. Civilization, Modern—21st
century—Philosophy. 3. Civil society—Philosophy. 4. Europe
—Civilization—21th century. I. Title. II. Series.
HM451.087 2006
301'.094—dc22
2005020271

A catalogue record for this title is available from the British Library.

Set in 11.5/13.5pt Bembo
by Graphicraft Limited, Hong Kong
Printed and bound in the United Kingdom
by TJ International Ltd, Padstow, Cornwall

The publisher's policy is to use permanent paper from mills that operate a sustainable
forestry policy, and which has been manufactured from pulp processed using acid-free
and elementary chlorine-free practices. Furthermore, the publisher ensures that the text
paper and cover board used have met acceptable environmental accreditation standards.

For further information on
Blackwell Publishing, visit our website:
www.blackwellpublishing.com

Contents

Contents

PART III Implications

Preface

This book is not a work of futurology,[1] and in particular it is not about the prospect that human beings might cease to live in a social way. Such a prospect is inconceivable. The question is rather about the nature of our social relations, and whether these relations continue and will continue to be shaped by processes and ideas centered on what people came to call society or societies. This use of the term "society" dates from around the seventeenth and eighteenth centuries in Europe; it has a beginning, and therefore might also have an end.

Since around the last third of the twentieth century there has been a growing sense that the concept of society is in danger of obsolescence; some would say it is already obsolete. It has always been a problematic term, and in the late twentieth and early twenty-first centuries it has been exposed to a new wave of critical attacks. Neo-liberals have polemically denied its existence: Margaret Thatcher famously claimed in 1987 that "There is no such thing as society. There are individual men and women, and there are families."[2] Postmodern theorists, notably Jean Baudrillard, have announced the dissolution of society into vaguer notions of "the masses,"[3] and theorists of globalization such as John Urry have argued the concept of society cannot survive the eclipse of the nation-state which was its implicit basis.[4] Evolutionary psychology and evolutionary sociology have suggested the replacement of the human model of society with conceptions more continuous with the social patterns of other animal species. Finally, more judicious commentators have traced the rise and fall of "society" as a concept in the social sciences (Peter Wagner) or its "forgetting" (Michel Freitag), and others have explored ways of avoiding it (Thomas Schwinn) or reformulating it (François Dubet and Danilo Martuccelli).[5] The concept of society, and perhaps society itself, are, to borrow the title of Zygmunt Bauman's recent book (2002), "under siege."[6] Paradoxically, however, we have seen at the same time a revival of uncritical notions of "the" economy, community, the polity, governance, democracy, and so on.

This book traces some of these controversies, arguing that, as Mark Twain said of newspaper reports of his death, reports of the death of society have been greatly exaggerated. We still live, I shall argue, in something that can usefully be called society, and we participate in interlocked *societies* at various levels. Our societies are different from animal societies in very many ways, but one important difference is that we have come to have relatively explicit *representations* of our societies which help to sustain them.[7] Society in the singular, conceived as a particular form of association or sociation, I shall argue, is not just an idea, a collective representation in Emile Durkheim's sense, but it is also that, as well, and the representation forms an important part of its reality and its causal powers.

We have not always thought about society in this rather abstract way, and the first chapter of this book explores the emergence of the concept of society. I then move on to examine various overlapping critiques of the concept of society, before considering ways in which we can construct a defensible concept of society (and civil society) and apply them to aspects of contemporary reality, notably the ongoing process of European integration.

Acknowledgements

I have presented versions of this argument at the University of Sussex, including the 2001 meeting of the International Consortium of Social Theory Programs, at the Universities of Brighton and Kent, at University College, Dublin, and the European University Institute in Florence. My thanks to all those who contributed at these sessions; John Holmwood and Peter Wagner, in particular, have heard this more often than is reasonable. Thanks also to Daniel Chernilo for some exceptionally helpful comments on a draft of this manuscript, and to the anonymous readers for Blackwell. Also to Laura Marcus, whose conversation with my old friend Andrew McNeillie led to the proposal for this book, and to Ken Provencher of Blackwell, for whom this is my third book.

For Daniel

1

The Origins of "Society"

How did people come to use terms like "society," and how did they think about what we now call society? First, and most importantly, many cultures, including that of medieval Europe, tend to represent human society as part of a cosmic order. Ancient Chinese thought, for example, was shaped by an imperial frame of reference in which the "middle kingdom" was not just the center of the world but a central part of a natural harmony which could be disturbed by human agency.[1]

In ancient Greek thought, and particularly in Aristotle's very influential formulation of it, the primary contrast is between human association or community (*koinonia*), culminating in the political community or state (*polis*), and the private individual or household (*oikos*). The former is naturally prior to the latter, as the whole is prior to its parts. There are two things to note about this conception. First, what we now tend to differentiate as the social and the political are not distinguished here; when Aristotle calls man a "political animal" (*zoon politikon*), the term can as easily be translated as social.[2] Second, the assumption of the priority of the whole over the parts is one which some later social and political theorists also see as naturally correct but others as fundamentally mistaken. This tension runs right through discussions of society (and more explicit political oppositions) up to the present. Anyone who stresses the shaping of individuals by society or the explanatory primacy of the social or collective is liable to be accused of a potentially tyrannical or totalitarian lack of concern for the individual, as in liberal critiques of "collectivism."

Aristotle, it seems safe to say, did not suffer critiques of this kind, and although Christianity, that strange hybrid of Jewish and Greek thought, introduced a dualism between the civil and the religious or divine community, these were intended to be in harmony with one another. A similar set of conceptions to the Chinese ones mentioned earlier can be found in medieval European Christianity.

A more secular and abstract conception of society and, with it, the state, comes into existence in Europe at the time of the Renaissance and, more substantially, in the "long" Enlightenment of the seventeenth and eighteenth centuries.[3] "State," "état" or "stato" come to mean something more than a state of affairs, a distinction still marked in the German language, which was consolidated only at this time, in that between "Staat" and "Zustand" – a condition or state of affairs. "Society," similarly, congeals from a vague notion of association, as in "the society of one's fellows," into a more structured conception of what is sometimes called civil society, existing in some variously conceptualized relation to the emergent state. As Keith Michael Baker summarizes the French context:

> It seems clear from the dictionaries . . . that a critical shift in the meaning of *société* occurs at the end of the seventeenth century.
>
> The earlier, voluntaristic associations of the term with partnership, companionability and civility do not disappear; but they are joined by a more general meaning of society as the basic form of collective human existence, at once natural to human beings and instituted by them, a corollary of human needs and a human response to those needs.[4]

The tension over the issue of whether society and the political in this sense should be seen as natural or an artificial construction is worked out in part initially through the historical thought-experiment of social contract theory. As David Frisby and Derek Sayer showed in their excellent book on the concept of society,[5] this tension runs through the work of thinkers such as Hobbes in the mid-seventeenth century and Rousseau (who famously wrote about a state of nature which, he said, probably never existed)[6] and Montesquieu in the mid-eighteenth. By the end of this period, however, Montesquieu believed that the argument was largely won, though people might need to be "reminded" that they lived in a society and were "confined" by law to their mutual obligations.[7]

Montesquieu, however, was of course writing in France.[8] In Germany, the term society was still associated with the rise of the bourgeoisie and an object of suspicion to conservatives right through the nineteenth century and well into the twentieth. Bluntschli's dictionary referred to "society" as a "concept of the third estate,"[9] and in 1859 the conservative historian Heinrich von Treitschke published a substantial pre-emptive critique of the idea of a science of society.[10] This defense of "state science" (*Staatswissenschaft*) against social science and sociology was interestingly replayed in the 1950s, the early years of the Federal Republic, in an attack from political science on the "new" concept of political sociology.[11]

In the Scottish Enlightenment, by contrast, Montesquieu's robust defense of the concept of society was warmly welcomed by Dugald Stewart and others, and their conceptions strikingly anticipate much of the analysis of Marx and Engels in the mid-to-late nineteenth century. Marx and Engels tend to speak of "social relations" rather than "society" – a conception which they see as too imprecise. As Marx put it, in an important methodological fragment of 1857, "To regard society as one single subject [*Subjekt*] is . . . to look at it wrongly, speculatively."[12] He goes on to elucidate this in a discussion of "The Method of Political Economy":

The economists of the seventeenth century . . . always begin with the living whole, with population, nation, state, several states etc.; but they always conclude by discovering through analysis a small number of determinant, abstract, general relations such as division of labour, money, value etc. As soon as these individual moments had been more or less firmly established and abstracted, there began the economic systems, which ascended from the simple relations, such as labour, division of labour, need, exchange value, to the level of the state, exchange between nations and the world market. The latter is obviously the scientifically correct method. The concrete is concrete because it is the concentration of many determinations, hence unity of the diverse.[13]

But Marx also emphasizes the importance of society as a frame of reference for more specific investigations. A little later in the same text, he writes:

> In the succession of the economic categories, as in any other historical, social science, it must not be forgotten that the subject, – here, modern bourgeois society – is always what is given, in the head as well as in reality, and that these categories therefore express the forms of being, the characteristics of existence, and often only individual sides of this specific society, this subject [*Subjekt*].[14]

The nineteenth century also saw the development of more substantialist conceptions of society in at least three ways. First, a more ethnic or even "*völkisch*" conception of nationality increasingly replaced the universalistic and civic conception of the French Revolutionary thinkers, in which "nation" is more a class term than a territorial or ethnic one.[15] Second, conservative defences of community opposed both capitalism and its emergent socialist and communist critics. The complex associations between social science or sociology (the latter term invented by Auguste Comte in the 1830s), on the one hand, and "the social question" or socialism, on the other, form an ongoing political background to theoretical debates right through to the Thatcherite attack on British social science in the 1980s.[16] More fundamentally, as Peter Wagner has shown, the discussion of society and social science is in large part an exercise in political theory and a reconceptualization of relations between the individual or the private sphere and the state (see Chapter 5).

Finally, biological analogies became popular in the work of Herbert Spencer (1820–1903) and a number of central European writers such as Albert Schaeffle, Ottmar Spann and Ludwig Gumplowicz.

"A society is an organism," said Spencer,[17] and he went on to draw analogies between the nervous system and the new networks of communication such as telegraph wires.[18] These conceptions mutated (to use another biological analogy) into the structural-functional system theories of the mid-twentieth century.

The formative years of sociology as an academic specialism were the decades just before and after the end of the nineteenth century. Of the leading sociological thinkers of that period, five can be taken to illustrate the main conceptual reference points which have remained salient for more recent discussions. We should look first at Emile Durkheim (1858–1917), the most explicitly sociological and society-focused of this generation. Durkheim was, if one counts Tocqueville and Comte as precursors, the founder of sociology in France; he was certainly its institutional founder. He wrote a charter for the subject: the famous *Rules of Sociological Method* (1895),[19] followed by a pioneering study of *Suicide*[20] which aimed to show, by analyzing the regularities and regular variations in suicide rates, that high rates could be explained by an insufficient or, in other cases, excessive degree of social integration and regulation. Suicide was, however, like other forms of deviant behavior, a normal feature of a society or social species operating, like an organism, within certain parameters.

Durkheim had earlier used similar terminology in differentiating between normal and abnormal forms of the division of labor in society.[21] "Undoubtedly society is a being, a person," he had written in 1885, in an early review of Gumplowicz, and if his language later became a little more cautious and precise, he stuck to this original intuition.[22] Suicide, crime, the division of labor, industrial conflict, and so on are all products of a certain state of society. Even religion turns out neither to be a simple illusion, since it is too substantial for that, nor to be about supernatural entities (assuming they do not exist), but rather about society – the form in which societies conceptualize, celebrate and reinforce their solidarity. A society, for Durkheim, is not exactly an organism, but it is very like one in having emergent properties not reducible to those of its component parts, in its forms of integration, its operating parameters which map out its normal and pathological states, and so on.

All this must be heavily qualified by Durkheim's equally strong insistence on the importance of what he called collective representations.[23] In his early work on the division of labor, he had referred to the "*conscience collective*," the collective conscience or consciousness,[24] in connection with the "mechanical solidarity" of what he considered simpler societies without a developed division of labor. In his subsequent work, this notion mutates into a broader set of concepts variously designated as *conscience commune, conscience sociale,* and *représentations collectives.* There is considerable ambiguity in Durkheim's thinking about just what ontological or causal status these have. At times, notably in his occasional references to Marxist materialism, they seem secondary to structural or morphological social relations.[25] Elsewhere, they seem to be primary. He claimed in *Suicide* that "social life is entirely made up of representations"[26] and complained in a preface to the second edition of the *Rules of Sociological Method,* that "Although we have expressly said and repeated in every way that social life was entirely made of representation, we have been accused of eliminating the mental element from sociology."[27]

As Sue Stedman Jones points out, "It is clear that in claiming that society consists entirely in collective representations, a social system is a conceptual and discursive system."[28] Whether or not this was really Durkheim's intention, there can be no doubt of the importance of the concept of representations in his thought, and in particular his conceptualization of society. As he put it in a lecture on moral education, "Society is not the product of the individuals included in it at this or that phase of history."[29]

But whatever the make-up of society in Durkheim's conception, it is clear that he treats it as an independent variable, a material and efficient cause of a whole variety of social processes. It is this which repelled many of his contemporaries and has continued to worry many of his readers. As the British social anthropologist E.E. Evans-Pritchard wrote, in his critique of Durkheim's theory of religion, "It was Durkheim and not the savage who made society into a god."

At the other extreme from Durkheim is someone who would not have called himself, and is not often considered to be, a sociologist, Friedrich Nietzsche (1844–1900). I include him in this context because his conceptions of cultural criticism and of the heroic individual were so influential on social theorists of the most diverse political persuasions. The three thinkers who unquestionably do count as sociologists, Ferdinand Tönnies (1855–1936), Georg Simmel (1858–1918) and Max Weber (1864–1920), are hard to imagine without Nietzsche's influence. Tönnies and Simmel both published important works on Nietzsche and what Tönnies called the *Nietzsche Cult*,[30] and Weber famously commented on the fundamental importance of Marx and Nietzsche for himself and all his contemporaries. Nietzsche opposed sociology and feminism, yet his work was influential for both.[31]

Georg Simmel's conception of society is directly contrary to Durkheim's. He rejects any notion of society as a substantial entity, focusing instead on forms of interaction and a more abstract principle of sociation (*Vergesellschaftung*) discussed in more detail in Chapter 6. In a kind of sociological version of Kant, Simmel answers the Kantian question: "How is society possible?" with reference to the synthesizing activities of members of society themselves. "The consciousness of constituting with others a unity is all there is to that unity."[32]

Simmel's version of Nietzschean *Kulturkritik* takes the form of what he called "the tragedy of culture"[33] – the tendency for cultural innovations to be routinized and to lose their creative character. Max Weber also makes a rather broader concept of culture central to his own thinking. In a fundamental rejection of substantial conceptions of society, Weber avoids the term almost entirely, preferring verbal forms such as sociation (*Vergesellschaftung*) and community-formation (*Vergemeinschaftung*). He wrote in a letter to Robert Liefmann: "If I have become a sociologist . . . it is in order to put an end to the use of collective concepts."[34] For Weber, a sociological (as opposed to legal) concept of, say, the state can only mean the probability that a certain number of individuals typically orient their behavior to such an idea, by obeying laws, paying taxes, joining armies, and so forth.

Weber's sociology is a sociology of action, not society – the polar opposite in theory at least, to Durkheim's. In our time they would be constantly asked to debate their positions with one another. A hundred years ago, they barely noted each other's existence.[35]

For Weber, the rejection of holistic models of society and of a "conceptual realism" (*Begriffsrealismus*) or, as we would now say, "reification," which he identified with Hegel and Marx and their followers, was a main starting-point in his own methodological reflection, documented in an early critique of the nineteenth-century historical economists, Roscher and Knies.[36] He did not directly criticize his contemporary, Durkheim's, society-based sociology, though he can hardly have been sympathetic to it. Weber's approach was, however, greatly influenced by his friend Georg Simmel, whose earlier works on *Social Differentiation* (1890), *The Problems of the Philosophy of History* (1892), *Moral Philosophy* (1892–93) and *Sociology* (1908) he acknowledges at various points in his own work.[37] For Simmel, whose more positive reflections I shall discuss in Chapter 6,

> What palpably exists is indeed only individual human beings and their circumstances and activities: therefore, the task can only be to understand them. Whereas the essence of society, that emerges purely through an ideal synthesis and is never to be grasped, should not form the object of reflection that is directed towards the investigation of reality.[38]

Weber wholeheartedly agreed with this approach, insisting that a sociological, as distinct from a legal conception of a state or a community could only be formulated in terms of the probability that individuals would orient their action in relation to it: "What motives determine and lead the individual members and participants in this ... community to behave in such a way that the community came into being in the first place and continues to exist?"[39]

In contrasting *Vergemeinschaftung* and *Vergesellschaftung*, Weber was reworking Tönnies's classic distinction between "community" (*Gemeinschaft*) and "society" or, as it is sometimes translated,

8

"association" (*Gesellschaft*). In *Gemeinschaft und Gesellschaft* (1887), Tönnies contrasted the small-scale, intimate, face-to-face relations of (typically rural) communities with the large-scale, anonymous, bureaucratized and monetarized relations of the modern city. Here, "society" becomes a conception of a particular type of social interaction. Tönnies was fundamentally ambiguous about his evaluation of these two types. His ostensible aim was to employ them in a neutral or value-free manner as polar types, but his language constantly suggests the kind of critique of modern society which was common on the political right and to some extent also the left, where Tönnies's own attachments lay.[40]

I have spent some time presenting these classical sociological and related conceptions of society both because they have been influential in their own right and because they illustrate the major conceptual options available to later thinkers in the twentieth and twenty-first centuries. Holistic conceptions are carried forward in structural functionalist and system theories, notably by Talcott Parsons and Robert Merton in the USA and later by Niklas Luhmann in Germany, individualistic approaches in rational choice theory, most creatively by Jon Elster and Martin Hollis, and a more group-centered conception in action theories such as that of Alain Touraine and his sociology of social movements. Simmel's influence continues in phenomenological and social constructionist theories which stress the constitution of society by and in our representations of it. As we shall see, these theoretical approaches all conceptualize society differently.

First, however, we need to set these more academic theories of society against the broader social context of European politics and thought. As we saw in the passage from Marx quoted above, he was concerned, both as a theorist and as a revolutionary activist, to analyze and exploit the internal divisions within societies – notably, of course, those between classes. The first major section of *The Communist Manifesto* which Marx and Engels wrote in 1848 begins with the ringing phrase: "The history of all previous societies is the story of class struggles."[41]

As Marx said,[42] he did not discover the model of class division which was central to his analysis both of capitalism and, a bit more tentatively, of human history as a whole. It can be found in ancient Greek and Renaissance thought and had been increasingly used by nineteenth-century French historians in explaining social change. Analyses of "society," as we saw in the previous pages, can be holistic, like Durkheim's, or individualistic, like Weber's. They can also differ in their representations of society between approaches which we can call monistic and ones which are dualistic or pluralistic. Marx's model in the Manifesto is essentially a dualistic one, which he re-states in the posthumously published Volume III of *Capital*:

> The specific economic form in which unpaid labour is pumped out of the direct producers determines the relation of rulers and ruled, as it grows immediately out of production itself and reacts upon it as a determining element . . . The form of this relation between rulers and ruled naturally corresponds always with a definite state in the development of the methods of labour and of its productive social power.[43]

In other works, Marx analyzes these "empirical circumstances" in more detail. His basic model of capitalism is still dualistic, polarized between the bourgeoisie and the proletariat, though he notes the existence of a residual independent peasantry and petty bourgeoisie which he sees as destined to fall into the proletariat. Other social divisions or cleavages: ethnic, religious, national, and so on, are, in the end, merely a distraction from the principal antagonism between bourgeoisie and proletariat which is grounded in capitalist relations of production. The practical conclusion is the organization of a workers' international movement: "Proletarians of all countries, unite!" Elsewhere, though, in his writing on the history of France, Marx draws much finer gradations between classes and political alignments in a model which one might even call pluralist.

Max Weber too was concerned to analyze class divisions, though he sees them as only one basis of division in modern societies. He was also a nationalist, and his approach to class conflict in contemporary Germany was shaped as much as anything by the thoroughly un-Marxist question of what class was best suited to provide national leadership. (His answer, as it happened, was the bourgeoisie.) Durkheim's principal focus, by contrast, is on society as a whole, and his politics are closer to the welfarist solidarism of the French Third Republic.

As Jacques Donzelot[44] has shown, the rise of social policy in France was essentially an attempt to defuse a political challenge from the "popular classes." In Germany, Bismarck expanded welfare provision in the 1880s, while the newly founded Socialist Party was banned from 1870 to 1890. In Britain, the "social question" was framed in similar, though somewhat more charity-centered and less political terms ("No class conflict please; we're British"). This difference of emphasis remains today in the contrast between British and French state responses to social exclusion. In Britain, which only picked up the slogan of exclusion (which had been in use in academic discussion for some time) when the Blair government was elected in 1997, exclusion is seen primarily as a welfare problem. In France, it is represented as a potential threat to the health and well-being of the harmonious Republic of citizens.[45]

In party politics, the last three decades of the nineteenth century saw the rise of social democracy, with the foundation in 1869 of the German SPD and in 1900 of the British Labour Party. By 1906, the German sociologist Werner Sombart was raising what came to be a standard question about a form of American exceptionalism in asking "Why is there no socialism in the United States?"[46]; five years later Robert Michels was recording and regretting the bureaucratization of the SPD.[47] Both later made the fateful move from extreme left to extreme right, in Germany and Italy respectively.[48]

The mutation of democracy into social democracy shaped politics inside Europe and, to quite an extent, outside it, for most of the twentieth century; it is only in the late twentieth century that one finds an explicit return by many thinkers to a post-socialist vocabulary of radical democracy.[49] In Western Europe after 1945, social and

Christian democracy (and, in France, Gaullism) concurred in moderate welfarist policies funded by post-war economic prosperity.

What of the political extremes of the twentieth century? Fascism and Communism differed of course in the way they conceived the state and society. The fascists and the Nazis explicitly invoked the total state,[50] embellished in Nazism with the neo-conservative and anti-socialist concept of the "people's community" (*Volksgemeinschaft*). Under communism, by contrast, the state was intended ultimately to wither away or die off (*absterben*)[51] in favor of the self-organization of society. In practice, of course, the state rapidly became even more omnipresent than under fascism and Nazism; the trade unions and other "mass organizations" became mere transmission belts for the party-state. Civil society, in the sense of autonomous associational life, existed, so far as it did at all, in the interstices of the official systems or in secret. The movements of the 1980s were in large part movements of civil society, and they gave the concept the resonance which it still has today (see Chapter 7).

We left academic social theory around 1920, the year of Max Weber's death, with the paradox that, of the "founding fathers" of Weber's generation, only Durkheim defended an emphatic concept of society. The others, in different ways, advanced more modest ideas of sociation in which "society" appears as the outcome of processes of interaction and social constitution (Weber and Simmel) or as a specifically modern form of association (Tönnies). More holistic and substantialist models of society bounced back in the following decades in the form of structural functionalism.

The social anthropologists, Bronislaw Malinowski (1884–1942) and A.R. Radcliffe-Brown (1881–1955), were confronted with relatively clearly delimited societies which largely lacked written records. Durkheim had been careful to distinguish between the historical and causal explanation of a social process such as the division of labour, and a functionalist account of its beneficial social consequences for the society as a whole.[52] In ethnographic field-work, where the former was impossible, it was natural to rely on the latter. As Radcliffe-Brown put it: "An institution may be said to have its

12

general *raison d'être* (sociological origin) and its particular *raison d'être* (historical origin). The first is for the sociologist or social anthropologist to discover."[53]

Social institutions could therefore be "explained" by their contribution to meeting the needs of society, as well as those of its component individuals. It may seem uncontroversial to define institutions in functional terms, in which, say, the family assures the reproduction of the population and the socialization of young people, the legal system regulates social relations, and so on; to say what something is very often is to say what it does. Later, when this approach had been taken up in general sociology by Talcott Parsons, Robert Merton and others, it was sometimes suggested that it was not a specific theory of social life, or a method of approaching its study, but simply *the* sociological approach.[54]

Critics, however, poured cold water on the conception of a harmoniously integrated society intuiting its alleged needs and ensuring, by invisible means, that they were met. If the way back to Spencer's organic analogies was blocked,[55] more abstract notions of system seemed the modern alternative, but the relation between the "system integration" of the component parts of societies – the neatness of the "fit" between them – and "social integration" by means of shared values and legal and political norms (which was also central to functionalist theorems) was unclear.[56] Were there really sound criteria of social health, well-being, sickness and death of the kind familiar to physicians? Were societies not conflictual as much as consensual?[57] Was functionalist system theory not a rather conservative approach to social life?[58]

There were of course possible responses to these objections, but social theories (and many natural scientific theories too) succumb not to testing and refutation, as in textbook methodology, but more to changes in intellectual fashion loosely linked to other changes outside as well as inside the relevant scientific community. As the relative social harmony in "the West" in the 1950s (albeit accompanied by the threat of nuclear war and the reality of several conventional wars) gave way to conflicts at home, with the student and counter-cultural protest movement waves of the 1960s, structural-functionalism and system theory seemed out of date, especially in the English-speaking countries, where they had been strongest. (In continental Europe, and especially in Germany, there was a more serious and continuing engagement with system theory.)

What alternative ways of thinking about society were available? The most prominent was in approaches which denied its necessity altogether. Empirical social researchers could study specific social processes without reference to a concept of society, just as astronomers and biologists moved away from common-sense reference-points such as "the sky" or "life."[59] Rational action theorists, discussed in more detail in the following chapter, argued that large-scale societal processes could be explained at the level of individual motivation. Interactionists focused more on small-scale social processes and treated the societal context merely as a background to processes of self-presentation which were very similar in their underlying orientation, even if their specific details were different in different types of society. Action theories, as again we shall see later, continued to develop in a rather ambivalent relation to conceptions of society. Finally, postmodern social theory, repeating certain moves previously made in social constructionist sociology, broke through into the consciousness of late twentieth-century populations with a radical questioning of intellectual and social order (see Chapter 3). With the themes of neo-liberalism, postmodernity and globalization, academic philosophy and social theory again converge more directly with public discourse.

PART I
Critiques of Society

2

Society and the Individual
Neo-liberalism, social constructionism and communitarianism

There is no such thing as society. There are individual men and women, and there are families.

(Margaret Thatcher)[1]

This chapter examines the interrelations between a number of distinct positions in social and political theory which may seem to have little in common beyond their rejection of conceptions of society or social structure. I shall suggest, however, that there are affinities between them, notably in the most explicitly political version represented by Thatcherism, which brings together neo-liberal individualism and the apparently opposed conceptions of what we have come to know as communitarianism.

As we saw in the previous chapter, European conservatives were initially suspicious of the concept of society, and the more romantic idea of community has always had more appeal. However, the idea of a human society stretching over a long time frame and implicitly conceived in national and territorial terms ("la terre et ses morts") is also an intrinsically attractive one to conservatives. In Britain, "Our Island Story,"[2] the title of a popular history book for children, was jokingly relabelled as "our island's Tory"; "national" is still used in Europe as a euphemistic self-description for the extreme right. Social theory was indeed using concepts of conservative origin, as

17

Robert Nisbet argued in an influential book,[3] even if, as his critics pointed out, the use it made of them was more often liberal and progressive.

The Christian democracy which dominated Western Europe after the Second World War became the modal political formation. In the late 1950s and early 1960s, British Conservatism under the relatively progressive Harold Macmillan, French Gaullism and even German and other versions of social democracy were increasingly assimilated to this model; on the left, the West German SPD relabelled itself a people's party (*Volkspartei*) and the British Labour Party nearly made a similar move away from its socialist rhetoric.

In the UK this convergence was labeled Butskellism, after two leading politicians who narrowly missed the premiership, the long-serving Conservative economics minister, Rab Butler, and the Labour leader, Hugh Gaitskell, whose unsuccessful attempt to "modernize" the Party's image according to the SPD model was taken up in a more muted form by his successor, Harold Wilson, and finally came to fruition 30 years later under the leadership of Tony Blair. Although the Labour left, closer to what on the Continent had come to be called Eurocommunism, grumbled about the centrism of post-war politics, the real challenge came from the Conservative right, which in the 1970s, responding in part to the oil price shock and the recession and spending cuts of 1973, developed an unstable but potent combination of neo-liberal economic and social theory and traditional social conservatism. Thatcherism swept the Party and the country, and continues to haunt other parts of Europe and to some extent the rest of the world.

The quotation from Thatcher at the beginning of this chapter makes a convenient peg for the discussion, but the stress on obligations shows that her ideology was not consistently neo-liberal. Even Friedrich von Hayek, the ultimate source of many of her ideas, had a quite developed conception of society as a spontaneous order emerging from and underlying the actions and representations of the human beings who participate in and sustain it. Hayek was primarily concerned to argue against scientism in social theory and social engineering in political practice;[4] a free society is one which is free from rationalistic attempts to manipulate it. For a sharper critique, we must go into more strongly individualistic programmes of the kind which Hayek saw as excessively rationalistic. The economic paradigms of rational action and rational choice offer a way in.

Economic theory from the late nineteenth century onwards has attempted to get by with a vestigially thin conception of the social framework. All the work in its explanations is performed by rationally motivated individuals. The American economist, Gary Becker,[5] is one of the most uncompromising defenders of this conception. Practices such as marriage, child-bearing and prayer do not require complicated and sensitive cultural explanations involving an interpretive understanding of human beings; all we need is a model based on simple assumptions about intentionality, rationality and available information against the background assumption that, as Hume put it a couple of centuries earlier, "mankind are so much the same, in all times and places."[6]

A model of this kind can be used to explain collective action, as in Mancur Olsen's work[7] and in "rational choice Marxism," and to reconceptualize issues in the analysis of social structure, as attempted by James Coleman,[8] and fundamental issues in philosophy and social theory, notably by Martin Hollis and Jon Elster. Hollis, in *Models of Man*, presented a powerful defense of "autonomous man," whose "rational action is its own explanation."[9] Hollis's co-authored book with Steve Smith is a friendly battle between his position and other, more structural conceptions of explanation, represented by Smith.[10]

Rational action theorists differ on the question whether people consciously think and behave rationally most of the time ("internalism"), or whether it is just that they behave as if they do, perhaps from unconscious habit ("externalism"). Becker's approach, he writes, "does not assume that decision units are necessarily conscious of their efforts to maximize or can verbalize or otherwise describe in an informative way reasons for the systematic patterns in their behavior."[11] Most of the time rational action theorists, despite paying lip service to ideas of testability and falsification, offer explanations which, like others in the social sciences, are really *post hoc* redesciptions. They also tend, as Göran Therborn notes,[12] to trade on a common sense based on local evidence. Crucial tests to decide between the merits of rationalistic and culturalist explanations in ethnographic research or in the study of social movements are conspicuous by their absence; what we are offered instead is the choice between quasi-transcendental interpretive frameworks.

As usual, when there is a choice between alternative theories and no obvious way of deciding between them, social theorists shift to the level of metatheory, replaying philosophical oppositions between realism and nominalism, individualism and holism. The neo–liberal critique has its main philosophical basis in methodological individualism, the claim that explanations of social phenomena should be in terms of individuals. This, however, tends, as Steven Lukes showed in his very useful book on *Individualism*, to be associated with ontological individualism, the doctrine that only individuals are real, and individualism as a political philosophy.

We might start with what Lukes characterized and criticized as "truistic social atomism":

> Society consists of people. Groups consist of people. Institutions consist of people plus rules and roles. Rules are followed (or alternatively not followed) by people and roles are filled by people. Also there are traditions, customs, ideologies, kinship systems, languages: these are ways people act, think and talk.[13]

Truisms are of course true, and there is enough truth to this one to put the burden of proof on those who wish to assert the existence of something other than people and extensionally specified groups of people (the people in this room, the people who have bought this book, the people who live in Britain, etc.). The diversity of ways in which society or social structure have been conceptualized means that these concepts present quite an easy target for sceptics.[14] On the other hand, it is not at all clear that one can in practice operate an individualistic reduction of causal explanations without getting into unnecessarily cumbersome circumlocutions: to unpack a statement about, say, the Wehrmacht invading Poland in September 1939 into a list of names of military personnel and registration numbers of vehicles is as absurd as trying to describe my computer molecule by molecule.

At this point, of course, neo-liberals can reach for a strategy borrowed from the philosopher, Hans Vaihinger (1852–1933), and his philosophy of "as-if,"[15] thus borrowing the clothes more often worn by conventionalist defenders of the concepts of society or social structure. Whereas these defenses have sometimes suggested that the use of holistic or structural concepts in the social sciences should, as the twentieth-century French sociologist, Pierre Bourdieu put it, always be preceded by an implicit "Everything happens as if . . . ,"[16] neo-liberals can argue that although there probably *are* societies and perhaps even classes, and so forth, we should act as if they did not exist, heroically pursuing our enlightened self-interest in the teeth of social conventions and pressures. The more we do this, the more the baleful influence of society, and with it perhaps social democracy, will wither away.

The neo-liberal critique tends to equivocate between an outright rejection of "society" as a collectivist illusion and a claim that there *used to be* various undesirable forms of social determination in earlier forms of society but that they are on the way to extinction in the bright dawn of the open society. As we shall see, something of this tension between a historical and a transhistorical thesis can also be found more broadly in, for example, Max Weber's concept of "disenchantment" (*Entzauberung*), in the contemporary French sociologist Alain Touraine's concept of "historicity" or in temporal, as opposed to epistemic conceptions of postmodernity (i.e. where it is seen as an epoch succeeding modernity, rather than a sceptical moment which coexists with it and may even predate it). For Weber, opposition to holistic concepts in social science, which, as we saw in the last chapter, he once memorably claimed to have been a main reason for his becoming a sociologist, was clearly part of what he saw as a mature response to the disenchantment of the world and

21

the loss of old certainties. For Touraine, similarly, the "strength" of historicity seems to mean the degree to which society is, and is perceived to be, a human product.[17] A sociology of action, as Touraine sees it, is the form of sociology which fits advanced industrial or post-industrial societies. (This motif is also strong in the postmodern conceptualizations discussed in the next chapter.)

The slide between historical and transhistorical versions of individualism and critiques of society intersects with that between ontological and methodological individualism. The relations between them are not so much entailments as what Weber called "elective affinities." If, for example, humans have become more individualistic, because of capitalism, secularization, postmodernity or whatever, it may sort of follow that our explanations should be framed more in terms of individual motivation than in reference to social wholes (though maybe they should be anyway). If social structures are fictions, it sort of follows that we should not use them in our explanations, though they might still be argued to have a use as shorthand expressions to describe aggregate effects.

Observing from the sidelines, the sociologist of (scientific) knowledge comments that the more individualistic the social scientist (or his/her culture), the more s/he will be drawn to individualistic explanations – rather like the legendary animal experiments in which rats studied by British psychologists sought food mainly by trial and error, while those in German labs were alleged to work out rational strategies from first principles. Thus, while philosophers and other careful analysts of argumentation will wish to differentiate sharply between logical or conceptual and psychological or historical arguments, in practice, we should not be surprised to see more syncretic mixtures. Arguments are a bit like cocktails, remaining recognizably the same as the exact proportions of the individual components vary according to chance or taste.

It makes sense, clearly, to begin with the ontological and methodological versions of individualism before looking at attempts to historicize them. Let us begin with the ontological version, as addressed in the quotation from Lukes. This combines what he calls

22

truistic social atomism with the further claim that it is only the people or individuals who are real; the structures are in some sense fictional or have at best a second-order reality as clusters of people. Individuals are normally independently viable; Robinson Crusoe (minus Man Friday) is a real possibility.

Explanatorily, too, the level of individual human action seems to have a kind of priority. That I am writing these words here and now or that you are reading them some time later has a kind of bedrock status despite the possibility of reductionist physiological explanations of the processes underlying writing or reading, or more structuralist accounts of the way in which writing and reading are aspects of the reproduction of certain sorts of discourse. Individuals are physically separate, except in the limiting case of "Siamese" twins, whereas social structures and institutions, assuming they exist, are interlocking and overlapping. This is true even in terms of their composition: the same person can be, and invariably is, a member of a whole number of structural sets (a family, an extensionally specified collectivity such as the class of people with red hair or American Express cards, or more concrete ones such as organizations). It is also true of more theoretical entities: if I see a power elite in contemporary Britain and you see a ruling class, our conceptions may be defined in opposition to one another or seen simply as intersecting. What is less clear is what follows from this.

Some theorists, as different in other respects as Hayek and Karl Popper, on the one hand, and Rom Harré, on the other, want to make the further move of saying that social structures or wholes are merely representations. For Hayek:

> The social sciences . . . do not deal with "given" wholes but their task is to constitute these wholes by constructing models from the familiar elements – models which reproduce the structure of relationships between some of the many phenomena which we always simultaneously observe in real life. This is no less true of the popular concepts of social wholes which are represented by the terms current in ordinary language; they too refer to mental models.[18]

For Karl Popper, too, "social entities such as institutions or associations [are] abstract models constructed to interpret certain selected abstract relations between individuals."[19] Note the curious way in which Popper seems to blur the differences between a manifestly theoretical category such as "the British bourgeoisie" and an institution such as the London School of Economics, where he worked for much of his life. Only someone with a substantial theoretical ax to grind would move so quickly from truism to paradox.

More recently, Rom Harré has expressed a radical and transhistorical skepticism about all social structures, and *a fortiori* about societies. Harré, whose approach in social psychology is a form of social or discursive constructionism, has defended for many years an increasingly sceptical view of social structures, while upholding a philosophical realism about science in general which inspired and continues to resemble that developed by Roy Bhaskar and others.

In *Social Being* (1979), Harré writes:

> In the social sciences facts, *at the level at which we experience them*, are wholly the creation of theorizing, of interpreting. Realists in social science hold, and I would share their belief, that there are global patterns in the behaviour of men in groups, though . . . we have no adequate inductive method of finding them out.[20]

Around the same time, in an unpublished paper entitled "Images of Society and Social Icons," Harré wrote:

> According to the view which I wish to advocate, society and the institutions within a society are not to be conceived as independent existents, *of* which we conceive icons. Rather, they *are* icons which are described in explanations of certain problematic situations. Thus, the *concept* of a Trade Union, or a University, is to be treated as a theoretical concept judged by its explanatory power, rather than a descriptive concept judged by its conformity to an independent reality. The form of a social and a scientific explanation are identical, but their ontological commitments and metaphysical structures are quite different. Beyond the icons of reality which are conceived for

24

purposes of explanation in the natural sciences, lies a real world of active things; but beyond the icons conceived for the explanation of social interactions by social actions lies nothing but those very actors, their conformative behaviour and their ideas.

By the end of the twentieth century, Harré's tone is sharper[21] but his argument is, ostensibly at least, methodological rather than onto-logical.[22] "I am not saying that there no such 'somethings' as social structures, but they are not the right kind of 'something' to do the work that some Critical Realists would like them to do."[23] His argument is essentially that what we call social structures or institutions, whether extensionally or intensionally defined, are ultimately reducible to the actions and interactions of people, and statements about them should be thus reducible, on pain of reification in analysis and evasion of responsibility in practical contexts. For Harré, "the efficacious agents in the social world are people. They are shaping their world. They are creating the social structures in which they falsely believe themselves to be fatally enmeshed."[24]

In a more recent contribution, Harré[25] frames his argument in a discussion of the realist notion of causality, to which of course he had made a fundamental original contribution in the 1960s. He distinguishes between "event causality," "where we take the causal relation to be between events . . . [and] . . . agent causality, the idea of a continuously existing being, continuously active which can bring about events without being stimulated in any way."

The question, then, is which of these conceptions applies to social structures. Harré gives the example of gravity to illustrate the latter conception, and he later draws out the implication that social structures, if they exist, would have to operate according to this model. "Quite plainly the causal ontology of events will not apply in the social case just because a social structure, though composed of events [*sic*], is not an event."[26]

Apart from the dubious assertion that social structures are composed of events, this is surely right. The effects of a demographic, linguistic, or class structure must be taken to operate in an ongoing manner, even if, like the effects of natural fields such as gravity, they can be counteracted by other forces, as when we experience weightlessness diving in a plane. Even where the effect is momentary, as when an illegal move in computer chess is punished with a beep, the underlying rule structure built into the software is permanently present. Harré goes on to differentiate two sorts of thing identified by uses of the term "social structure": first, "institutions," such as a family or the Third Reich and, second, "rules and conventions." In both cases it is individual persons who perform structural roles or follow (or break) the rules and conventions. "The people play the roles and thus *they generate the structure.*"[27]

This is a familiar area of controversy,[28] and I shall confine myself here to some short comments. My main point is that Harré's insistence on conceptualizing social relations in terms of the way they present themselves to us is unduly restrictive, and that he himself has frequently adopted a more sophisticated approach.

In what I find an extremely illuminating passage in *Social Being*, Harré addresses the issue of properties such as role which "is experienced, not as a relational property in which the individual stands to the collectives of which he or she forms a member, but rather as a systematic set of psychological and microsocial imperatives and constraints."[29] This differentiation of the concept of role, as individually experienced imperatives, on the one hand, and structural position, on the other, is I think extremely useful, but it is not clear to me why Harré apparently believes that the more abstract concept is not also accessible to actors.

To understand the imperative aspect of role, one might say, necessarily includes a more complex relational conception in which the bearers of different roles interact in a variety of ways. I may experience my role as author as, say, an imperative to complete my book on time, but this obligation necessarily involves an understanding of the complex interdependencies and constraints of book production. And one can and must meaningfully distinguish the interrelations between formally specified roles from the concrete interactions between incumbents. This distinction, familiar in studies

26

of bureaucracy but also central to any social theory, was described by David Lockwood in 1964 in his classic distinction between system integration and social integration, respectively.

Lockwood was identifying an ambiguity in functionalist social theory, but the implications of his distinction are a good deal broader. To put it briefly, system integration and social integration are analytically and socially distinct, and may vary independently. The occupants of badly co-ordinated formal social positions may, for example, get things done by informal cooperation, as they often did in state socialist planning systems. Conversely, system integration in, say, markets, may occur with only the most minimal degree of social cooperation between the participants.[30]

Harré can, of course, respond by again invoking the societal icon concept, seen now as a reference-point for the cognitive activities of role-bearers in their *conceptualizations* of social structure. There are, of course, precedents for this, as in Max Weber's classic contrast in the opening pages of *Economy and Society* between juridical and sociological conceptions of the state, where the latter denotes "a specific complex of collective human action whereby the actions of particular people are governed by their belief that it exists or should exist."[31]

To anticipate an argument which I shall make later, in Chapter 6, this is, however, to load the dice in favor of a cognitivist model of societies and other social structures, where I would prefer to treat it as an empirical question how far the ontological constitution or make-up of social relations depends upon certain conceptions existing in the heads of those concerned. Even in areas of inquiry quintessentially concerned with belief, sociologists of religion, for example, argue about the relative importance of beliefs on the one hand and habitual practices on the other in sustaining religious communities.[32] Is capitalism or state power preserved mainly by ideological means or by some other processes? Did state socialism collapse mainly because of declining growth rates or other macro-structural properties or because of its failure to sustain its ideological credibility in the minds of its citizens? We don't know *a priori*, and we shouldn't prejudge such issues.[33]

Social or discursive constructionism of the kind which underlies
Harré's approach has its origin, of course, in Peter Berger and
Thomas Luckmann's classic book of 1966, which offered in the
guise of a sociology of knowledge a conception of society drawing on
phenomenological philosophy, mediated by the Austrian philosopher
and sociologist Alfred Schutz, and the work of Simmel and Bergson.
For Berger and Luckmann, "society as an objective reality" is the
product of processes of definition and conceptualization. They were
explicitly relativistic in their approach, arguing that the sociology of
knowledge should be concerned with "whatever passes for 'knowledge' in a society."[34] Society, though socially constructed, is, however, both an objective and a subjective reality.[35] Again, this can be
illustrated by the notion of role:

> Looked at from the perspective of the institutional order, the roles
> appear as institutional representations and mediations of the institu-
> tionally objectivated aggregates of knowledge. Looked at from the
> perspective of the several roles, each role carries with it a socially
> defined appendage of knowledge ... The first perspective can be
> summed up in the proposition that society exists only as individuals
> are conscious of it, the second in the proposition that individual
> consciousness is socially constructed.[36]

Berger and Luckmann see themselves, then, as mediating between
Weberian and Durkheimian approaches;[37] more recent social constructionism has tended to drop the latter aspect. In sociology,
"ethnomethodology," the study of the way we produce order in
everyday life, where it did not immerse itself in detailed sociolin-
guistic studies, developed into more speculative philosophical reflections, often drawing on Heidegger. More generally, the theme of
social construction has come to be associated with postmodernism,
where its more sceptical emphasis finds a comfortable home. At the
same time, as we shall see, Durkheimian motifs have returned in
communitarian models (which Durkheim would probably have hated)
and have inspired conceptions of social policy in which individuals

are increasingly made responsible both for their individual welfare and for that of the ideologized national community. This has in turn given rise to a new line of analysis, discussed later in this chapter. In studies, substantially inspired by Michel Foucault, of representations of the social and the state, we can find a more powerful notion of social or discursive construction.[38]

There is of course a substantial gap between suggesting doubts about the sceptical critiques of the very possibility of social structures, and a defence of a particular structure, let alone one so ambitious as "society." Ontological individualism is in any case less common than the more muted doctrine of *methodological* individualism, of the kind discussed above (pp. 20ff.) in relation to Becker. This doctrine, which can also of course be found in Harré's earlier writings cited above, claims that, whether or not there *are* social structures or other collective entities, explanations should always be cast in terms of individuals, their motives and their actions. Social predicates are more or less pre-loaded into the social context and/or the actors (William, university professor and author, went to the bank to pay in his check from Blackwell because it was getting close to Christmas and the mail was unreliable . . .), but the working bit of the explanation is always individual. Structural shifts, such as that from the use of checks to electronic bank transfers, are ultimately reducible to specific decisions of private individuals or (individuals in) organizations.

In practice, this tends to mean a reference to *typical* individual actions, where the actors are *typical* bearers of roles in organizations, rather than involving a careful examination of them one by one. At this point, of course, critics tend to suggest that the explanation has ceased to be individualistic in any substantial sense, and that all that is left is a preference at the margin for more individualistic rather than more structural explanations.

This preference in turn is underpinned by the appeal of rational action models. The models themselves bifurcate into the more automatic, almost behavioristic versions favored by most economists, and the gentler versions which link rational action to understanding. Finally, these two approaches to rational action have affinities to

29

different conceptions of individualism – the former tied to utility maximization, typically in markets, while the latter displays a broader concern with individual human autonomy.

In liberal democracies such as the UK in the 1970s, individualism in the broad sense of respect for individual liberties and rights was, of course, the shared currency of political discourse, so it was economic liberalism that provided the *differentia specifica* of Thatcherite conservatism. For mainstream Thatcherites, however, as distinct from the extreme liberals who favored the free circulation of hard drugs and private currencies, there was always an implicit reference back to, if not society, at least the "nation" or the "community." Although Thatcher might not have put it quite like this, this is clearly the entity to which, along with ourselves and our "neighbors," we have duties and obligations, and in whose name she made war on Argentina and the British coal miners.

Communitarianism

Neo-liberalism, indeed, coexisted at this time, in social and political theory and also in political practice, with what came to be called communitarianism. As we saw in the previous chapter, community had long been presented as the cuddly alternative to, or alter ego of, society. It was not at the center of the first wave of communitarian social and political philosophy in the 1980s, which was animated more by a critique of liberal individualism, focusing on its self-interested psychology and its neglect of the embeddedness of people in social and cultural structures. Alasdair MacIntyre's *After Virtue* (1979) was an influential contribution, followed by Charles Taylor's *Sources of the Self* (1989), Michael Sandel's *Liberalism and the Limits of Justice* (1982) and Michael Walzer's *Spheres of Justice* (1983).[39]

A more Durkheimian conception of community emerged in the work of sociological communitarians in the 1990s, following the publication of Robert Bellah et al.'s influential *Habits of the Heart: Individualism and Commitment in American Life* (1986) and *The Good*

30

Society (1991).[40] Another sociologist, Amitai Etzioni, popularized "responsive communitarianism"[41] outside the academy in a series of books in the 1990s, and communitarian ideas can be seen in the thinking and practice of center-left political leaders such as Clinton and Blair and some of the thinking parts of the center-right, notably in Germany and for a time also in the UK, as the Conservative Party relocated in the early years of the twenty-first century to compete with Blairism on a "caring" agenda. For a time it seemed as if communitarianism might become the dominant mode of political discourse in the twenty-first century, flanked by residual socialist parties and movements and a right made up of old-style authoritarians such as Jean-Marie Le Pen and postmodern showmen like Pim Fortuyn and Silvio Berlusconi. The new extremism of George Bush II's Republicanism and British Conservatism currently suggest that this is less likely, though it still seems a realistic prospect for parts of continental Europe.

The formal doctrine of comunitarianism, such as it is, has had relatively little appeal to European intellectuals, except as a correction to liberalism. They tend to find its rhetoric vapid and the concept of community imprecise and "of little analytic value."[42] The US, where organized religion has survived better than in Europe, seems a more fertile ground for this sort of thing. It is, however, interesting that "community" remains a more marketable concept than "society," and the concept has played an important role in the reconceptualization of social policy. Nikolas Rose has brilliantly described some of the outlines of this transformation, contrasting the current focus on community with earlier modes of social governance.[43] In a new administrative logic, the aim is no longer to reintegrate problematic individuals and populations into a social totality focused on the state, as to push them, discretely, into individual strategies of self-improvement and provision for ill-health, old age, and so on:

> The person who is to be made prudent is no longer mutualized but autonomized.[44]

With this new territory of exclusion, the social logics of welfare bureaucracies are replaced by new logics of competition, market segmentation and service management: the management of misery and misfortune can become, once more, a potentially profitable activity.[45]

At the same time, populations that resist or are unresponsive to these strategies are demonized as inhabitants of "wild" or "savage" zones of cities or territories:

We can thus be governed *through* our allegiance to particular communities of morality and identity. Many programmes of government now operate upon the presupposition of such communities, even where the allegiances presupposed do not immediately appear to exist.[46]

Another, and I think complementary, way of explaining this vogue for the notion of community is perhaps that it enables one to take on board the fragmentation of modern or "postmodern" social, political and cultural relations, seen as undercutting earlier models of society, while leaving open the possibility of a kind of redemption through community. This makes rhetorical sense, however unconvincing it may be politically or sociologically; indeed, it replays many of the tropes familiar from the previous *fin de siècle* and the early decades of the twentieth century, notably in the response to Tönnies.

Why, you may wonder, am I displaying such an aversion to the concept of community, which has long been a perfectly serviceable element in the repertoire of sociological concepts?[47] My main objection is that it is generally used to figure an idealized and unpolitical conception of unity among people who are more appropriately conceived in a more differentiated way. A particularly crass example of this is in conventional representations of ethnicity and/or religion in Britain, in frequent references to "the black community," "the Asian community," "the Muslim community" or, in Northern Ireland, "the Protestant/Catholic communities." Here, an essentially colonialist discourse suggests the existence of homogeneous populations, represented by "community leaders" as *interlocuteurs valables* of the colonizing metropolitan power. There are parallels with what is conventionally (and of course not unproblematically) characterized as "ethnic" as opposed to "civic" nationalism, the emphasis is on a pre-political and somehow more primordial attachment. Beyond this, the imagery seems to be merely ideological, as in "community policing" or "community care."[48]

This chapter began with various relatively extreme forms of individualism and has ended up discussing discursive interactionism and communitarianism. There is, I think, an underlying connection – a dialectic, if you like – in which individualism produces its opposite to complement it.[49] The kind of position represented by Rom Harré and other discursive constructionists is a very different matter. Harré is clearly not a methodological individualist, since it takes two to discourse, and usually more if one is to have anything like a rich discursive community. (Here even Crusoe *plus* Friday is a bit limited.) On the other hand, by restricting himself to what he used to call act–action structures and discursive events, he ends up with a position similar to that of many methodological individualists, for whom social structures exist, again, only as intentional objects. The stress on individual actors and their ethical responsibilities makes his position closer to an individualist one than any other discussed here. I can imagine a possible world in which Harré is *also* a postmodernist, but this is not, I think, a label he would want to attach to himself, and nor would I want to pin it on him. But the boundaries between his sort of position and the sort of social constructionism which anticipates postmodernism is an open and shifting one which it would be a mistake to try to mark out too precisely. (The same goes, as we shall see in Chapter 5, for the relation between postmodern and globalist critiques of the concept of society).

3

Postmodernism

Postmodern theory in the social sciences began with a critique of "grand narratives." In Jean-François Lyotard's classic formulation, "I would argue that the project of modernity (the realization of universality) has not been forsaken or forgotten but destroyed, 'liquidated'."[1] Whether or not Lyotard's own thesis, as stated above, itself falls within the scope of this critique, narratives of the development of "society" clearly do so. Where everything, including "social relations," is shifting and fluid, there can clearly be no place for a concept of society of the kind defended in this book. As Lyotard put it a little earlier, in the book which initiated postmodernism in social theory, *The Postmodern Condition*:

> economic "redeployment" in the current phase of capitalism . . . goes hand in hand with a change in the function of the State: the image of society this syndrome suggests necessitates a serious revision of the alternative approaches considered.
>
> What is new in all this is that the old poles of attraction represented by nation-states, parties, professions, institutions, and historical traditions are losing their attraction.[2]

As Rojek and Turner summarize the postmodernist[3] sociologist Jean Baudrillard's critique of Michel Foucault, "The society to which Foucault ascribed solidity, weight and depth is, for Baudrillard, elastic and transparent."[4] This is, indeed, something like the standard

34

postmodern position, whether one thinks of the kind of postmodern thinkers emphasizing epistemic skepticism or those celebrating a more playful social world beyond the discipline of modernity. The French-Canadian sociologist, Pauline Marie Rosenau, usefully differentiates between these two admittedly overlapping and cross-cutting strands of postmodern thought:

> the skeptical post-modernists . . . argue that the post-modern age is one of fragmentation, disintegration, malaise, meaninglessness, a vagueness or even absence of moral parameters and societal chaos . . .
>
> . . . the affirmative postmodernists . . . have a more hopeful, optimistic view of the post-modern age . . . They are either open to positive political action (struggle and resistance) or content with the recognition of visionary, celebratory personal nondogmatic projects that range from New Age religion to New Wave life-styles and include a whole spectrum of post-modern social movements.[5]

Postmodernists of the first type tend to speak of the death of society or, as we shall see, of the social; those of the second type tend to accentuate the positive: the emergence of new forms of sociality – what Michel Maffesoli has called the dionysiac or the neo-tribal.[6] It is interesting, however, to note that, whereas the critiques we examined in the previous chapters have mostly rejected what they see as substantivistic conceptions of society in favor of weaker notions of sociation or social relations, where the social appears in an adjectival form, Baudrillard directs his skepticism at the concept of "the social" rather than society:

> there have been *societies without the social*, just as there have been societies without history. Networks of symbolic ties were precisely neither "relational" nor "social". At the other end, our society is perhaps in the process of putting an end to the social, of burying the social beneath a simulation of the social.
>
> Only "sociology" can seem to testify to its agelessness, and the supreme gibberish of the "social sciences" will still echo it long after its disappearance.[7]

As Baudrillard puts it in another text, "sociology cannot but describe the expansion of the social and its vicissitudes. It survives only on the positive and definitive hypothesis of the social. The reabsorption, the implosion of the social, escapes it."[8]

It seems clear, however, that what Baudrillard understands by the social is something like what has been meant by analytical, as distinct from purely descriptive, uses of "society." "The social," Baudrillard suggests, is a kind of perspectival or panoptical space which locates objects in relation to one another. But this "comedy of errors" "is only one simulation model among others." "Ultimately, things have never functioned socially, but symbolically, magically, irrationally, etc."[9]

> End of the perspective space of the social. The rational sociality of the contract, dialectical sociality (that of the State and civil society, of public and private, of the social and the individual) gives way to the sociality of contact.[10]

It is perhaps (he presents many of these suggestions in the form of "hypotheses") not so much that the social has died, as that it is already a kind of death, an "excremental"[11] "residue" like "value in the economic order, the phantasm in the psychic order, meaning in the order of language."[12] "Symbolic integration is replaced by functional integration,"[13] rather as, in the sexual sphere, seduction solidifies in sexual relations and exchange.[14]

Drawing together the threads of this vigorous, though hardly rigorous, *dérive*, it seems that Baudrillard is contrasting the static notion of society or the social with a more dynamic, fluid and symbolically mediated notion of sociality. The concept of the social, even if it never had a real referent, had a kind of historicity at least as a representation. It now finds its end in the shadow of silent majorities and in the banal concept of "social relations."[15]

Gilles Lipovetsky continues the same line of reflection in *L'ère du vide: essais sur l'individualisme contemporain*:

> The great axes of modernity, revolution, discipline, lay society and the avant-garde, are disaffected by the powerful current of personalist hedonism . . . No political ideology is capable of inflaming the crowds, for postmodern society no longer has either idols or taboos, it no longer has a glorious image of itself, nor a mobilising historical project; it is a void that rules us, but a void without tragedy or apocalypse.[16]

Postmodernity means "the predominance of the individual over the universal, of psychology over ideology, of communication over politicization, of diversity over homogeneity, of the permissive over the coercive."[17] Like Baudrillard, Lipovetsky makes society or "our societies" the backdrop to this "second individualist revolution":

> Negatively, the process of personalization relates to the fracturing of socialization by discipline; positively, it corresponds to the mode of operation of a flexible society based on information and the stimulation of needs, sex and the incorporation of "human factors," the cult of the natural, of cordiality and humour.[18]

Michel Maffesoli, in a related approach, has developed the notion of society as sociality, tracing it theoretically back to Simmel and forward to a reflection on subcultural neo-tribalism in modern societies. Sociality is intrinsically (and increasingly) playful, dionysiac and far removed from the Durkheimian severity of more traditional models of society. "In reflecting too much about *society* and the purely rational, intentional or economic elements which constitute it, we have left aside *sociality*, which is something like a *communalized empathy*."[19]

This approach, he stresses, does not deny the value of specialized sociological research but wishes merely to complement it with a general sociology, with the qualification that this should aim less at "discovering a 'hidden meaning' of existence than at the understanding of the societal 'affirmation.'"[20]

Maffesoli stresses the dionysiac theme in Nietzsche. The Nietzschean motif can of course be pushed in another direction, with the suggestion that the death of society or the social (as traditionally conceived) repeats the death of God celebrated by Nietzsche.[21] Arthur Kroker[22] notes the closeness of Baudrillard's language to Nietzsche's – for example in the parallel between Baudrillard's silent majorities and Nietzsche's "last men." In Bryan Turner's analysis, postmodernism reflects a challenge to the hegemony of bourgeois European *culture*, and thus has an underlying affinity with the decolonization process and postcolonial critique.[23] "The inability of Marxism and sociology to analyze culture opened up a space in modern social theory which has been occupied by postmodernism."[24] More positively, Nietzsche can be used to "bring sociology back to its origins, namely an exploration of fellowship (*socius*) through the analysis of reciprocity against the revenge of institutions and rationalism."[25]

In Baudrillard's more negative analysis, "the mass is what remains when the social has been entirely forgotten."[26] The motif of forgetting is also central to the Swiss-Canadian sociologist Michel Freitag's "critical theory of postmodernity" (the subtitle of *L'oubli de la société*). For Freitag, however, this postmodern experience is set against an insistence on the continued existence of society which his *œuvre* as a whole is concerned to analyze. Freitag attempts, he says, to do justice to what he calls two "intuitions":

> that of the real existence of *society* as a concrete and autonomous synthetic instance governing . . . the ensemble of the particular practices and social relations which it integrates in a totality which is at one and the same time "functional" and meaningful; secondly, that of the real, contemporary existence of a global change in the formal mode of constitution of society and of sociality.[27]

Freitag is, in Zygmunt Bauman's terms, a theorist *of* postmodernity rather than a postmodern theorist. He differs from postmodern theorists in presenting a "realist," "dialectical" and "ontological" account of what we might call a moderate conception of postmodernity, centered around the idea of fragmentation. Society increasingly appears as merely a "systemic environment for a set of separate entities," "impersonal organisational forms", linked to one another only by technical relations or by impersonal media such as the internet and pursuing limited strategic objectives. "It is . . . society itself which is tending to lose any synthetic, subjective and transcendental dimension, and which ceases to be representable as such."[28]

Bauman himself, whose version of postmodernity or what he now calls "light" or "liquid" modernity has also always been measured and reflective, offers a similar analysis of the loss of faith in society in more concrete terms:

> The image of society drew its credibility from the experience of collective constraint – but also from the sense of collective insurance against individual misfortune, brought about by the establishment of collectively sustained welfare provisions, and above all from the sense of the solidity and continuity of shared social institutions . . .
>
> . . . all three types of experience – of consistent normative pressure, of protection against the vagaries of individual fate, and of the majestic longevity of a collectively controlled order – began to fade fast in the last decades of the twentieth century and to be replaced by another experience, which no longer suggested a "company", but rather (to borrow Keith Tester's description) a world that was "separated from individuals", a world that "has experientially become increasingly like a seamless web of overlapping institutions with a independent existence."[29]

Bauman rightly stresses that these institutions have an uncertain life expectancy, and our everyday experience of takeovers and mergers of financial institutions, publishers, and so on confirms this. This type of institutional change is not a mere by-product of capitalist concentration or globalization. As Richard Sennett, Daniel Cohen and others have shown, it is explicitly pursued as a management strategy of control, and fueled by a legitimate tangentopoli of incentives. In Sennett's analysis, "perfectly viable businesses are gutted or abandoned, capable employees are set adrift rather than rewarded, simply because the organization must prove to the market that it is capable of change."[30]

At an individual level, what is required is a kind of entrepreneurship, flexibility and networking, rather than the traditional

39

white-collar employee's bureaucratically and hierarchically framed loyalty. Employees, as Cohen puts it, have to "demonstrate to the company that they have done their job well."[31] In practice, this will tend to mean meeting artificially set targets both for "performance" and for more tenuous interpersonal qualities of cooperativeness: "it is now the subjectivity of the worker which is at issue."[32]

A society whose organizational models increasingly take this form, not just in commercial enterprises but also in state administration, itself often hived off to quasi-independent agencies, will be not so much decentralized as decentered in its forms of self-representation:

> What seems to be gone . . . is the image of society as the "common property" of its members, which at least in principle can be conceivably tended to, run and managed in common; the belief that what each member does, or refrains from doing, matters – to the society as a whole and to all of its other members.[33]

Both Bauman and, so far as one can pin him down, Baudrillard, are committed to a historical thesis about the changing forms of social structuration and representation, even if, as Bauman puts it, society was always an "imagined entity."[34] What *has* changed is not just the paradigmatic forms of social organization and patterns of individual subjectivity, but the crucial link between society and the national state, which in most states tied a representation of society to one of the imagined national community. The globalization theorists discussed in the next chapter converge here with elements of what I have called the postmodern critique.

Before leaving the latter, however, I should say briefly what I find problematic about postmodernism.[35] My only real objections, apart from some aesthetic ones which I shall not bother to go into, are that it's not new and not true. Not new, because I do not believe that there is a clear divide between an earlier age, modern or at least pre-postmodern, and a postmodern condition prevailing since the last third of the twentieth century. The shock appeal of postmodern analyses derived largely from this chronological claim, made paradigmatically in Lyotard's slogan of the end of grand narratives. Postmodern*ism*, as it came to be known, was presented as not just a theoretical or metatheoretical option; it was allegedly underwritten by the movement of the advanced societies themselves towards a postmodern state. In Jean-François Lyotard's words, quoted at the beginning of this chapter, "I would argue that the project of modernity (the realization of universality) has not been forsaken or forgotten but destroyed, "liquidated.""[36]

Lyotard himself, however, more or less immediately backed away from this chronological claim, asserting the coexistence of modern and postmodern motifs and suggesting, rather irritatingly, that the postmodern could precede the modern as easily as follow it. Chronological postmodernism survived, however, in a shadowy way, like the Cheshire cat's grin, smirkingly insinuating that modernism and modernity were passé.[37] On the whole, however, it was the epistemically skeptical variant of postmodernism that took the strain and survives in a rather undifferentiated cocktail with "poststructuralism,"[38] deconstruction and antifoundationalism.

To say that postmodernism in the sense of epistemic skepticism is not new is hardly news: to say it's not true is not really entering into the spirit of the game. I shall, however, confine myself to the observation that the "social construction of reality," like W.I. Thomas's much earlier dictum that "if men define things as real, they are real in their consequences," had been largely assimilated into the mainstream of social scientific discourse, not least in the sociology of scientific knowledge. It was generally taken to entail a degree of methodological relativism, in the sense that it was bad form to say that one scientific theory supplanted another because it was better, just as it would be in the sociology of art or religion. But few people this side of the extreme fringe of ethnomethodology felt it necessary to assert the ultimate indeterminacy of everything and unknowability of anything – except in the weak sense of Popperian fallibilism or the realist stress on the open-ended character of science.

As I have argued more fully elsewhere, we should perhaps resist the appeal of what might be called the postmodern metaphor in the social sciences and scholarship as a whole, in which the non- or pre-postmodern is identified with modernist architecture and with its stress on function, order and system. The metaphor is seductive, if one thinks of closely argued multi-volume treatises in philosophy or sociology and the latter's indisputable connections to social policy and social engineering. But this captures only one aspect of philosophy and social theory: there is also a more tentative, questioning, exploratory aspect, which is more concerned with description and understanding than with formal demonstration and explanation, still less with prediction and control.[39]

In the philosophy of history and of the other social sciences, this contrast has traditionally been drawn between empiricism or positivism, on the one hand, and hermeneutic understanding, on the other. There is a good deal to this: in terms of the classical social theorists discussed in Chapter 1, above, one can see a line of division between a scientistic emphasis in Marx and Durkheim and the more tentative approach of Weber and particularly Simmel. Durkheim is the most obvious defendant here, with his sharp distinction between common sense and sociology and his bold claims that social facts should be treated as things and that one can distinguish between normal and pathological states of what he called social kinds or species (*espèces sociales*). In Durkheim's notorious conclusion to the *Rules*:

> as a preliminary condition for initiation into sociology, people are asked to discard concepts which they are in the habit of applying to a particular order of things, to rethink these things with new effort . . . We believe . . . that the time has come for sociology . . . to take on the esoteric character which befits all science.[40]

Even in Durkheim's work, however, the (if you like) modernist brutalism of the *Rules* fits oddly with much in his more speculative and tentative substantive works such as the *Elementary Forms of Religious Life*.[41]

The literature on postmodernism and postmodernity is substantially one of reviews, overviews, summings-up and even "postscripts";[42]

a postmodernist might even take this to be a vindication of the thesis of post-*histoire*. My sense of the outcome of these long debates is that the idea of a clear-cut separation, whether chronological or conceptual, between the modern and the postmodern has been largely abandoned. Ali Rattansi, for example, chose to put the term postmodern in scare quotes, thus "registering reservations about its distinctiveness and indicating a provisionality about its usefulness."[43] The editors of the volume in which this essay appeared express a similarly cautious view. While saying that for them, "and many contributors to this volume, the best available language was, and perhaps remains, that of postmodernism," and distinguishing between the modern and the postmodern in the way I have criticized, they argue for a "social postmodernism" which "integrates deconstruction while simultaneously incorporating some of the analytically synthesizing and expansive political hopes of the modernist tradition of social theorizing."[44]

In a similar vein, Rob Stones has argued for what he calls a "past-modern" sociology. Stones confronts the opposition between traditional, residually empiricist conceptions of scientific sociology and a "defeatist" post-modernist relativism stressing invention and style rather than substance. He identifies the former image of sociology with a variant of modernism, though he stresses how far it fell behind the sophisticated insights of artistic and literary modernism. His proposed alternative is based on two premises: a scientific realist ontology which upholds the reality of the social world, and what he calls a "past-modern" recognition of the complex issues raised by the attempt to describe and theorize it.[45]

More emphatically, a number of writers have argued, against postmodernism, that what we are experiencing is a process which is essentially continuous with modernity, confronting, perhaps, a second crisis, that of the welfare-state work society of advanced industrial civilization which was itself in part a response to the late nineteenth- and early twentieth-century crisis of the liberal polity. We are now faced, as, for instance, Claus Offe, Alain Touraine, Ulrich Beck and Peter Wagner have argued in various ways,[46] with the fragmentation

43

of many of these structures and their associated identities. More generally, Anton Zijderveld claims that "modern society has become abstract in the experience and consciousness of man." The abstract character of modern society is primarily the result of "segmentation of its institutional structure . . . As a result of this pluralism society has lost . . . much of its existential concreteness."[47] This is expressed not only in impersonal role relationships but also in abstract art-forms.

What remains of postmodern theory, in particular, is its challenge to earlier conceptions of modernity, in the form of mid-twentieth-century modernization theory and theories of industrial society. This, along with a postcolonial context of the provincialization of Europe,[48] its displacement from its previously hegemonic position, makes late twentieth-century theories of modernity substantially different from those a century earlier. They resemble them only in their scope, their historical range, and their opposition to the reductionist and scientistic economic and sociological theories of the mid-twentieth century.[49] I return to this body of thought in Chapter 6, following an examination of globalization theory and its critical relation to the concept of society.

4

Globalization

It is easy to forget how recent is the explicit discussion of globalization. Although of course elements of globalization theory are anticipated in classical Marxism,[1] in Marshall McLuhan's conception of the "global village" and its electronic media in the 1960s[2] and in Immanuel Wallerstein's neo-Marxist analysis of the capitalist world-system in the 1970s,[3] the term only came into use in the late 1980s, and most of the early contributions (such as those by Martin Albrow, Mike Featherstone, Anthony Giddens, Leslie Sklair, David Held and Roland Robertson) date from the 1990s.[4] It thus coincides with the rise of the personal computer and the early development of the internet – both of course powerful contributors to what came to be called globalization and dramatic metaphors for it. (As I write these lines, for example, I could within seconds convert them into an email message to be sent worldwide or, with only a little more effort, into a webpage accessible in principle to the whole world.) Globalization theory also of course overlaps with and reacts to the end of state socialism, of the Soviet Union, and of the bi-polar world.[5]

Globalization theory in any but its mildest forms entails a skeptical critique of the concept of the sovereign state,[6] and it is not surprising that this globalist critique tends to be extended to the concept of society. The American historical sociologist, Immanuel Wallerstein, in a paper of 1986 originally contributed to a conference on "Societal Development," sets the tone from his own "world-system" historical

45

perspective which anticipates much of later globalization theory. With accounts of society, he writes:

> we seem to be dealing with how some entity (an entity that is not the state, but also is not divorced from the state, and usually one sharing more or less the same boundaries as the state) has evolved over time from some lower to some higher or more complex level of being).[7]

> What is fundamentally wrong with the concept of society is that it reifies and therefore crystallizes social phenomena whose real significance lies not in their solidity but precisely in their fluidity and malleability.[8]

In Wallerstein's neo-Marxist analysis, it is the capitalist world-economy that has conjured up the nation-state system:

> It has been the world-system then and not the separate "societies" that has been "developing".[9]

> To contrast *Gemeinschaft* and *Gesellschaft* . . . is to miss the whole point. It is the modern world-system (that is, the capitalist world-economy whose political framework is the interstate system composed of sovereign states) which is the *Gesellschaft* within which our contractual obligations are located. To legitimate its structures, this *Gesellschaft* has not only destroyed the multiple *Gemeinschaften* that historically existed (which is the point normally stressed) but has created a network of new *Gemeinschaften* (and most notably, the nations, that is, the so-called societies.[10]

Despite Wallerstein's somewhat problematic Marxist functionalism in this necessarily compressed text, his main point is well taken, and converges interestingly both with more recent globalization theory and with other historical work concerned to deconstruct or traditional models of the "miraculous" development of Europe, wrongly taken in isolation from and placed in exaggerated contrast to the rest of the world.[11] Whatever important things happened at the western extremity of Eurasia in the second half of the last millennium, they must be seen in a broader historical and geographical context.

The British sociologist, Martin Albrow's theoretical allegiances are to Weber more than to Marx, but he differs from Weber and from many of the writers discussed in Chapter 5 in his belief that we have gone beyond modernity (and also postmodernity, which retains a definitional reference to modernity) in entering what he calls the Global Age.

> The dominant approach in this century [i.e. the twentieth] to the Modern Age has been to associate it with capitalism, industrialism or an abstract modernity and to regard the relationship of each to society as the key to understanding the course of events. "Capitalist society", "industrial society" and "modern society" have dominated writing about the Modern Age. Anything which looks like the decline or transformation of capitalism, industrialism or modernity is then seen as presaging a "post-age" in which society is in a dire state of disarray.[12]

The Modern Age, for Albrow (as, indeed, for most people), was the age of the nation–state. Much of social theory, he stresses, was "the voice of the nation-state . . . effectively designed to reflect back to the state its own efforts to control society."[13] In what he calls "The Decay of the Modern Project" (Chapter 3), some of its key elements became "forces for fragmentation: the corporate organization, the market, science, culture and the social (in the sense of social movements)."[14] All these came to transcend the boundaries of the nation–state even more radically than they had previously done, and to undermine it from within and without.

In a similar line of analysis, though one which, as we shall see, ends up at a rather different point, another British sociologist, John Urry, who has also been a major contributor to globalization theory, uses globalist theorems about the decline of the nation-state as a major element in his argument for "sociology beyond societies":

> The sociological concept of society is organised around the meta-phor of a region . . . Thus there appear to be different societies with their clustering of social institutions, and with a clear and policed border surrounding each society as region . . . globalisation fractures

this metaphor of society and hence problematises sociology's dominant discursive framework.

... globalisation involves replacing the metaphor of society as *region* with the metaphor of the global conceived of as *network* and as *fluid*... the global presupposes the metaphors of network and flow rather than that of region.[15]

There is undoubtedly a good deal of mileage in this focus on flows and networks, which captures important aspects of modern societies and organizations. Substantial numbers of people, for example, are in the air world-wide at any given moment, and many more are connected with and by global networks as they send emails, make telephone calls, or navigate their cars. Organizations are flatter, characterized less by formal hierarchies and chains of command and more by informal and impermanent task-based groups. Tasks such as the printing of this book are also increasingly contracted out by one core organization, in this case Blackwell, to a number of other companies or individuals. For my money, however, Urry's shift to a global ontology of mobilities, flows and scapes does not do justice to the continuing reality of societal institutions at national, subnational and supranational levels.

My previous book, for example, co-authored with Larry Ray, paid considerable attention to the impact of globalization on communist and post-communist societies but insisted on the very different national and regional contexts which make parts of the post-communist world no less radically different from one another, despite their historical connections until 1989/91, than, say, Canada and Kenya. As we wrote there, globalization and "path dependence"

did not lead directly to the neoliberal strategies of privatization, liberalization and marketization – these were strategic choices made in the context of the prevailing political and institutional climate. On the other hand the outcomes of these, where they were pursued ... were the result of configurations of local institutional and cultural conditions melded with global constraints and political strategies. The particular forms of capitalist development in parts of the post-communist world (such as the growth of insider capitalism, high levels of corruption and illicit dealing) attest to the importance not just of the rather vaguely formulated process of "glocalization" (i.e. the way in which globalization interacts with and may reinforce local diversities) but rather to the tolerance of the "global system" to multiple forms of local integration to it.[16]

A more nuanced discussion of globalization than Urry's can be found in Martin Albrow's analysis of the global age. We should, he insists, welcome its coming, as "the first period in human history when both sexes and all peoples have gone a substantial way towards asserting an equal right to make their contribution to the common stock of human knowledge."[17] Sociality has been liberated from the confines of the nation-state, as it has from unreflected tradition.[18] There is something like a world society, as an analogue of the world market, even though it is not yet, and may never be, global in the sense of explicitly world-focused and coordinated at a global level.[19] There is even, incipiently, a world state, in the sense of world-level political institutions, and a global state in the limited sense of individuals and groups orienting their political action to global issues and sites.[20]

A rather fuller argument along the same lines can be found in Martin Shaw's more recent book, *Theory of the Global State*.[21] As his title suggests, Shaw's version of globalization or, as he prefers to call it, globality, is as strong as they come, but he combines this with a judicious reflection on the categories of social analysis. Shaw's strategy of conceptual refinement, at the beginning of Part II of the book, basically takes the form of a set of moves from concretistic conceptions of society, culture, etc. to a more abstract set of models phrased in terms of levels which are constitutive of the social relations within them:

> Societies (or economies, or cultures) are those contexts of relations which are understood as *inclusive* and *constitutive* of social (or eco-nomic, or cultural) relations in general in a particular time and place. A society, economy or culture is a context of relations, by which other kinds of social, economic or cultural networks are seen as

49

being defined, or of which they are component parts . . . Conceptual discussion of societies, economies and cultures . . . has fallen out of favour, reflecting the greater interest in the open-endedness and dynamism of social relations . . . Clearly . . . we could reject such concepts altogether. We could argue that there are only social and cultural relations and multiple networks of such relations. We could then hold that to conceptualize these as relations within and between particular units is illusory and ideological because it reifies bound-aries. But this goes too far: social life has always been and still was informed by particularistic concepts. Boundaries, while relative, are real. Thus it makes partial sense of talk of, say, British, Kurdish or Zulu society, as well as many other networks and sub-cultures of sub-national and transnational kinds.[22]

Shaw's main theme, however, and the most contentious one, is that what we have experienced in the past 50 years or so is the emergence of what he begins by calling "the global Western state conglomerate" and rapidly ends up calling, more informally, "the Western state." This is the modern Global Prince whose advent, Shaw, following Machiavelli, and Gramsci's "Modern Prince," wishes to announce. The term "Western" is only contingently and in part geographical, since Shaw's Western state includes Australasia and Japan as well as its home base on the two sides of the North Atlantic. It was born, Shaw argues, out of the World War II anti-Axis alliance and the subsequent Cold War between NATO and the Warsaw Pact, in which the Soviet Union's place in the Western state was taken by the defeated enemies Germany, Italy (now linked in what has become the European Union) and Japan. It coexists, in the post-Cold War world, with what Shaw calls "quasi-imperial nation-states," on the one hand, (in which he includes not only Russia, China, and India but also a whole raft of medium-to-small established states, taking on the characteristics, including the militarism, of the traditional Euro-pean imperialist nation-state) and the "new, proto- or quasi-states" which have emerged or are emerging out of the other state forms.

Shaw's claims about the emergent global state, which I shall not discuss here, are paralleled by arguments of a similar kind which globalize the concept of society into images of a world society. As the German system theorist Niklas Luhmann put it in 1997:

> Under modern conditions, the global system is a society in which all internal boundaries can be contested and all solidarities shift. All internal boundaries depend upon the self-organization of subsystems and no longer on an "origin" in history or on the nature or logic of the encompassing system.
>
> Regional boundaries . . . are political conventions, relevant for the segmentary differentiation of the political subsystem of the global society. They designate places to show passports and, occasionally, generate reasons for war. It does not make any sense to say that they are separate societies.[23]

For Luhmann, then, the fundamental conceptual choice is between seeing the global system as "a society, or . . . [as] . . . a system of societies."[24]

In classical perspectives, one could compare the "degree of modernization" – say, of Japan and China – and explain their differences by different structural preconditions and semantic traditions. But when we want to observe the evolution of society, there is no other choice than to focus on the social system of the world society.[25]

The word "evolution" is of course not an innocent one and neither, in Luhmann's terminology, is the word "observation." It refers in a shorthand way to his system model and his conceptualization of the relations between the inside and the outside of such systems. Despite its remarkable sophistication, I do not find this model convincing and I shall not discuss it in more detail here. Nor am I convinced by Luhmann's suggestions, which he also makes in this context, that earlier models of society were led astray by the normative aspiration, which Luhmann calls utopian, of creating a better society and, as a separate though no doubt related point, that issues of stratification have lost their importance in the modern world.[26] His arguments for a world focus can, I think, stand in the absence of all this extra-theoretical and dubiously empirical baggage, though they would then become somewhat more tentative and closer to those of Martin Shaw. For Luhmann:

> In our context, where we have to decide between assuming a global system of regional societies or a world society, we . . . have clear and theoretically consistent arguments for a single world society. The autopoietic system of this society can be described without any reference to regional peculiarities. This certainly does not mean that these differences are of minor importance. But a sociological theory that wants to explain these differences should not introduce them as givens, that is, as independent variables: it should rather start with the assumption of a world society and then investigate how and why this society tends to maintain or even to increase regional inequalities. It is not very helpful to say that the Serbs are Serbs and therefore they make war. The relevant question is, rather, whether or not the form of the political state forced upon all regions on earth fits to all local and ethnic conditions, or, whether or not the general condition, not of exploitation or suppression but of global neglect, stimulates the search for political and social, ethnic or religious identities.[27]

Luhmann's system orientation no doubt leads him to reify the world society, just as earlier system theorists reified national state societies, and his nihilistic exclusion of any meaningful political options is discouraging, but his perspective remains an interesting one, as does Wallerstein's world-system analysis examined earlier. Theories of world society, of which Luhmann's is only one,[28] should probably be seen as a variant of theories of globalization. They tend to distinguish themselves from the latter, though to the extent that globalization theories have come to focus more on globality as a state of affairs rather than on the globalization *process*, the differences become less obvious.[29]

The strength of world society theory in any of these variants lies in its fundamental point that only the world is an unequivocally bounded unit of analysis: "The world society is the only social system that has fully unambiguous limits."[30] This basic orientation, and the notion that global inequalities should be seen as just that, as processes within a single system, are undoubtedly useful, both for historical studies of the rise and fall of world regions such as Europe and for the examination of contemporary global relations of production. Its weakness lies in its lack of precision and a tendency to overstatement.[31] Even to talk about large regional societies such as European society, as I do in Chapter 8, may be to stretch the concept of society to breaking-point. In the present context, however, the important point is that, far from globalization theory pointing inexorably to the abandonment of the concept of society, it can actually be taken to suggest that we look for sociation and societies at a variety of different levels, whether or not the world level is taken to be the primary or determining one.

PART II

Reconstructing Society

5

Modernity and Society

The idea of society is inseparable from a definition of modernity.
(*Dubet and Martuccelli*)[1]

Having looked in the last three chapters at critiques of the concept of society driven by fairly explicit theoretical commitments, such as empiricism, rational choice, postmodernism or globalization theory, I shall turn in this chapter to focus on more nuanced critiques of the concept of society. What links the thinkers discussed here is that their reflections on society are all shaped by an overall conception of modernity.[2] We last encountered modernity as the foil for postmodernism, but it also forms an essential background to conceptions of society, and I need to bring this out more explicitly.

Classical social theory was largely defined by its response to modernity, marked by a number of dualistic before-and-after conceptualizations. Henri de Saint-Simon, in 1825, distinguished between the ancient regime, dominated by clerics and court hangers-on, the first and second "estates" of the traditional social model, and the "industrial" or, as we should probably say, "productive" system. Alexis de Tocqueville distinguished a little later, in *Democracy in America* (1835/1840), between the old regime and democracy or the regime of the French Revolution. Both of course, were aristocrats by origin, and thus part of the outgoing order, while accommodating more or less readily to the new.[3] Marx and Engels, of course, wanted to go a good deal further, but their *Communist Manifesto* of 1848 presents a similarly dualistic contrast between the sleepy world

57

of pre-capitalist societies and the tough dynamic new world of capitalism (the *Manifesto* has been described as a hymn of praise to the bourgeoisie):

> The bourgeoisie, historically, has played a most revolutionary part . . .
> Constant revolutionizing of production, uninterrupted disturbance
> of all social conditions, everlasting uncertainty and agitation distin-
> guish the bourgeois epoch from all earlier ones. All fixed, fast frozen
> relations, with their train of ancient and venerable prejudices and
> opinions, are swept away, all new-formed ones become antiquated
> before they can ossify. All that is solid melts into air, all that is holy
> is profaned, and man is at last compelled to face with sober senses his
> real condition of life and his relations with his kind.[4]

Marx was not, he stressed, concerned to present the bourgeoisie as a class, or capitalists as members of that class, in what he called "rosy colors," but he saw capitalism as a necessary stage to be passed through – hence his remarks, which now may seem rather callous, about British rule in India. However brutal the British might have been, however devastating their impact on Indian societies, they built railway lines and so forth and that was a Good Thing.

Ferdinand Tönnies, in 1889, contrasted the small-scale, intimate, largely rural forms of pre-capitalist or pre-industrial society or community (*Gemeinschaft*) with the anonymous social relations of modern, urbanized *Gesellschaft*, bequeathing a typological contrast which has become one of the principal ways of thinking about different sorts of society.[5] Max Weber, once called the bourgeois Marx, also contrasts the traditional forms of economic activity with modern rational capitalism, in his classic account of *The Protestant Ethic and the Spirit of Capitalism* (1904/5): "One of the constitutive components of the modern capitalist spirit and, moreover, generally of modern civiliza-tion, was the rational organization of life on the basis of *the idea of the calling*."[6] Revisiting this contrast in the preface to his *Collected Essays in the Sociology of Religion*, Weber locates it in a general transformative process of Western rationalism: "the origin of economic rationalism depends not only on an advanced development of technology and law but also on the capacity and disposition of persons to *organize their lives* in a practical-rational manner."[7]

Emile Durkheim, Weber's contemporary, contrasted the "mechanical solidarity" of segmentary societies with the interdependent "organic solidarity" of societies with a more complex division of labor. Whereas in simpler societies of mechanical solidarity, "every consciousness beats as one,"[8] in conditions of organic solidarity, individuals can develop independently as well as interdependently, free of the "yoke of the common consciousness."[9] "It is the division of labour that is increasingly fulfilling the role that once fell to the common consciousness. This is mainly what holds together social entities in the higher types of society."[10]

These were all different ways of capturing the distinctiveness of what we would now call modernity – a way of life which emerged in Europe in a "long" eighteenth century stretching from the late seventeenth (or before) to the early nineteenth (or later) and which encompassed change both in the forces and relations of production and in demographic and spatial processes (notably urbanization) and in the relations among individuals and between them and the political structures in which they lived. If one has to reduce these complex changes to a single word, it should probably be individualism.[11]

Critics of this conception of modernity have rightly pointed to the dangers of focusing exclusively on Europe, rather than seeing it as a part of a broader Eurasian region and of an already significantly interdependent world, and on the more advanced regions and sectors within Europe, thus overlooking how slow, uneven and incomplete these transitions were.[12] It cannot, however, be denied that something significant of this kind happened in Western Europe and, by extension, the Americas and increasingly in much of the rest of the world.

In the mid-twentieth century, there was a tendency to concentrate on the broadly economic aspects of modernity and to neglect political (including geopolitical and military) and cultural processes. The theories of industrial society prominent in the late 1950s and early 1960s stressed the commonalities of industrial production and its consequences for social organization wherever it took place, and sometimes moved on to predict a convergence of all industrial societies towards a common pattern. The flourishing of Marxist social theory in the West in the aftermath of the 1968 protest wave also directed attention to the primacy of processes of production, even if this neo-Marxism rapidly shifted its focus to cultural processes. By the 1980s, however, the special prestige of Marxism had been relativized in favor of other, often equally longstanding, currents of social theory: Weberian, Durkheimian, and so on.

Generally, then, the time-perspective of sociology changed. Its substantive concerns once again became more historical, in a partial reversal of what the great historical sociologist Norbert Elias had attacked in 1983, a few years before his death, as "The Retreat of Sociologists into the Present"[13] – in other words, their excessive concentration on contemporary social phenomena. Sociology's sense of its own past also shifted. Anthony Giddens had attacked, in an influential article in 1972, what he called the "myth of the great divide" which had been set between the more or less unformed or chaotic pre-history of sociology and the subject in its modern "scientific" form.[14] This conception, he argued, involved both a lack of sensitivity to the work of the classical sociological thinkers and an undue degree of confidence in the scientific credentials of "our" social thought. Others came to share this more nuanced account of the continuities and discontinuities in social theory. Substantively, sociology shifted its theoretical focus from "industrialism" or "industrial society" to "capitalism" or "late capitalism" (*Spätkapitalismus* in West Germany, where the term was used by Habermas and many other theorists), and then to a broader focus on "modernity," in which it addressed dimensions of power (including state power in its international dimension) and culture, which had previously been somewhat marginal to its concerns.

To focus on modernity in this way was also to focus, reflexively, on social representations as not just reflections, more or less distorted, of real social relations, but as constitutive of those relations.

It made a real difference to class politics, for example, that French or Italian workers had access to an imagery of class and class struggle which North American workers on the whole did not. Alain Touraine's action sociology, discussed in more detail below, stressed the way in which social movements in modernity, or in what at the time he called societies dominated by historicity, were animated not just by particular individual or collective concerns but by a project of social transformation less all-encompassing, but on the same lines as, the Marxist one which had dominated many European and other labor movements. To think of society or social relations under conditions of modernity is to think of it/them not as grounded in the nature of things but as the outcome, more or less intended, of human action and more or less open to transformation by human action.

Charles Taylor, in a recent overview of Western modernity, brings out this dimension of what he calls modern social imaginaries. His use of the term, following Cornelius Castoriadis, Bronislaw Baczko and other writers based in France, is somewhere between concrete imagery and Lacan's more abstract Freudian notion:

> By social imaginary, I mean something much broader and deeper than the intellectual schemes people may entertain when they think about social reality in a disengaged mode. I am thinking, rather, of the ways people imagine their social existence, how they fit together with others, how things go on between them and their fellows, the expectations that are normally met, and the deeper normative notions and images that underlie these expectations.[15]

To stress the influence of these conceptions is not idealism:

> what we see in human history is ranges of human practices that are both . . . material practices carried out by human beings in space and time, and very often coercively maintained, and at the same time, self-conceptions, modes of understanding.[16]

In what he calls "the great disembedding," Taylor outlines the way in which people came to think of themselves as individuals: "our first self-understanding was deeply embedded in society. Our essential identity was as father, son and so on, and as a member of this tribe. Only later did we come to conceive of ourselves as free individuals first."[17]

Along with this changed self-conception come the ideas of the economy as a system, of a society objectified in the same sort of way, and of a public sphere and a self-governing people. The last two involve conceptions of collective agency; the former what Taylor calls a "bifocal" image: we can think of our society either in a way which includes ourselves or, in an "objectifying" account, as something operating according to its own laws: "this objectifying take on social life is just as much a part of the modern moral understanding, derived from the modern moral order, as the new modes of imagining social agency."[18]

This is, I think, an extremely illuminating observation. One might add that we move backwards and forwards between conceptions of these two kinds, and this is roughly what has been meant by people like Bourdieu and Giddens talking about reflexivity in advanced modernity. As Giddens stresses, borrowing a term from ethnomethodology, we have become knowledgeable about our social relations and social scientific knowledge is incorporated into our social representations. As Giddens puts it, "[A]nyone who gets married these days knows a great deal about marriage and divorce."[19] In thinking, for example, about environmental issues we will typically move back and forth between objectifying accounts of natural and social systems and their interrelations and a more personal and morally sensitive mode which recognizes our individual and collective implication in these processes. It would, of course, be easy to show that other cultures have and have had at least as acute an awareness of these interrelations, but it is probably still the case that the accentuation of both aspects in modernity enables us to think about them in a more precise way than in more, as one might say, automatically holistic formulations.

The three dimensions of society which Taylor distinguishes in the modern social imaginary: economy, public sphere and political system, are of course interdependent. In the case of the latter two, this is obvious, and Habermas has provided perhaps the richest and most inspiring account of their interrelations in a well-functioning democracy.[20] But the objectifying representation of economic, and, by extension, other social processes, is also an essential part of responsible citizenship and political action:

> Our modern imaginary thus includes not only categories that enable common action, but also categories of process and classification that happen or have their effects behind the backs of the agents . . .
>
> Grasping my society as an economy is precisely not grasping it as a collective action, but only because I understand the system in this way will I engage in market transactions the way I do. The system provides the environment my action needs to have the desired result . . .
>
> Active and objective categories play complementary roles in our lives.[21]

This dual perspective echoes two very different strands of social theory. The first comes from the speculative heights or depths of German philosophy. It is the metaphor of second nature or what is sometimes called "solidified" or objectified spirit. In this image, which has been watered down in the notion of unintended consequences or what Raymond Boudon has called "perverse effects,"[22] the products of human action come to take on an independent existence and to dominate their creators. We set up an organization and make ourselves into its puppets; we adopt an innovative artistic convention and find ourselves unacceptably constrained by it; we motivate ourselves with targets and pursue them irrespective of the purpose of what is being achieved. This motif is particularly strong in Max Weber's analysis of rationalization and bureaucracy and in his contemporary Georg Simmel's model of "the tragedy of culture." It pervades what Adorno and Horkheimer called "the Dialectic of (the) Enlightenment", in which the rational critique of tradition ends up in a form of domination through instrumental rationality and reverts to myth. The same theme returns in more formal sociological terms in Habermas' reworking of the Weberian rationalization theme in terms of Lukács's concept of reification. In Habermas' analysis, the rationality embodied in the critique of tradition and the development of rational legal structures opens up possibilities of communicative action, in which people come to an agreement on what should be done on the basis of rational arguments and reasons. At the same time, however, the development of markets and administrative bureaucracies undercut this possibility in virtue of their own procedures. The workers, as it were, can make a good case for a fairer share of the cake, but the "laws" of the market forbid capitalist generosity and the state rules their case out of court.

Habermas' distinction between the possibility of democratic and consensual decision-making on an informal basis in a rationalized lifeworld and the law-like operation of automatic systems is partly informed by the second theoretical element to which I wish to refer here: the distinction between system integration and social integration. This comes from a much less dramatic source, a classic paper, referred to earlier, in 1964 by the British sociologist David Lockwood, written to clarify an issue arising out of the functionalist theory which then dominated the USA and the UK.[23] The problem of integration is essentially the same as that which faced Durkheim: how is social order maintained if societies are not self-stabilizing in the same hidden-hand way as ideal markets and if the latter do not guarantee anything more than pragmatic cooperation driven by self-interest? Talcott Parsons,[24] who dramatized the issue as the "Hobbesian problem" of social order, argued that this was fortunately secured by a fundamental agreement in well-functioning human societies on a set of values and norms. What Lockwood pointed out was that the functionalists tended to equivocate between the language of technical integration of systems, the way in which their components fit together, and conceptions of social integration based upon more or less conscious agreements by individuals and groups of people. These, he argued, should be seen as distinct, and could function as alternatives to one another: "Whereas the problem of social integration focuses attention upon the orderly or conflictual relationships between the *actors*, the problem of system integration focuses on the orderly or conflictual relationships between the *parts* of a social system."[25]

This distinction has been very influential in sociology and more widely, in opening up a way of thinking of different ways of (as Habermas would put it) coordinating action. Very crudely, this can either be done by agreement, or by some form of market process or the adoption of a formal system of calculation. To take an example of a problem faced by my university and many others, we could respond to the shortage of car-parking space, assuming we do not wish this to be expanded, in two different ways. One would be to reach (and abide by) a collective agreement to use the car parks as little as possible, voluntarily leaving the spaces to those making long or difficult journeys, those carrying children, and so on. This would be one way of sharing out the space according to generally justifiable principles. The other solution, adopted as it happens by my economist vice-chancellor, is to impose a hefty charge for parking and vary it as necessary to prevent overcrowding. The former involves us in an orientation to general concerns and principles and to the reconciliation of competition in the light of common interests. The latter involves nothing more than an administrative arrangement and an individual decision about whether the cost is bearable and worth paying. Modernity involves the expansion of both sorts of practice, but with a perceptible slide towards the latter.

Behind these different orientations there is an even more fundamental feature of the modern condition. One way of interpreting it is to say that we are on our own: there is nothing outside our own societies which tells us how to order them. No religious or other system can prescribe our social and political arrangements. With the eclipse of explicitly religious justifications for European and North American social arrangements, there were two important further attempts to find an anchor for the social outside the social. One comes from the natural law tradition and is strongest in legal and political theory; the other derives from evolutionary theory and natural theology and finds a more congenial home in political

65

economy and then in the emergent science of sociology. By the end of the nineteenth century, both were largely out of the equation. Spencer's influential blend of evolutionary theory and market economics, with its assumption that self-equilibrating markets and commercial exchanges could of themselves sustain social solidarity, had been outflanked by something like the Durkheimian alternative, in which the organic solidarity of societies with a complex division of labor required a concept of society representing itself to itself in what he called the collective consciousness. A kind of evolutionism survived in the rather different form of Marxist philosophy of history, but it was more conditional and, as the twentieth century unfolded, increasingly pessimistic.[26]

The absence of extra-social guarantees for social arrangements is the starting-point for Alain Touraine's model of historicity and the self-production of society, where one can find a systematic reflection on what "society" might mean today. For Touraine, as mentioned briefly in Chapter 1, the "strength" of historicity means something like the degree to which society is, and is perceived to be, a human product. A sociology of action is therefore the form of sociology which best fits advanced industrial or post-industrial societies. Throughout his academic career, Alain Touraine has upheld a conception of sociology as the study of social action, in opposition to what he sees as the reification which tends to accompany the use of the term "society." Yet his is also a theory of society, or more precisely of the self-production of society, and he has become increasingly concerned about the opposite danger: the loss of all reference to society by sociologists and, more importantly, by social actors in general. On the one hand, Touraine has tirelessly attacked the concept of society as probably the most serious obstacle to the development of sociology today:

> Either it refers only to the totality of observable social facts within an institutional framework generally defined in administrative terms, which encourages every possible confusion between sociological and historical analyses, or it identifies a principle of the orientation of

66

behaviour and leads to an idealist interpretation, and above all an extreme impoverishment of research.[27]

This theme returns constantly in Touraine's work, both in his *Sociologie de l'Action*, cited above, and in a number of articles of the 1980s.[28] At the same time, however, Touraine writes repeatedly about the production of society or the action of society on itself; and he remains conscious, since his early stay in the USA, of the danger of a purely relational approach to action seen as interaction – an approach which lacks any reference to macrosocial issues.[29] In a move which recalls the approaches of Georg Simmel and Theodor Adorno, despite all their differences in intellectual tradition and orientation, Touraine rejects the reification of society as a substantive entity, "like a building,"[30] or identified with a concrete territorial entity.[31] But he insists no less on sociation and a constant reference to the social totality as a defining feature of social action. What sociology needs is a way of bridging the gap which he identified in his first major work "between the study of the elementary mechanisms of interaction and the description of massive ensembles such as societies, cultures, world-views or spirit of the time."[32]

Having established, in more or less complete form, his theoretical model predicated on the deconstruction of the concept of society, Touraine focused more and more in his subsequent writings on the conjunctural, as opposed to the theoretical importance of the concept of society in contemporary social thinking. In particular, one can detect a growing concern that the demolition of the concept of society should not be to the benefit of a state-centered perspective, which he sees as even more undesirable.

Touraine's focus on the concept of society comes out clearly in a volume of journal entries dating from 1974–76 and published under the provocative title *La Société invisible* (1977). As usual, Touraine starts with a bang on the first page: "Society has disappeared . . . On the one hand, we see nothing more than an economy growing or in crisis and international strategies; on the other, we react only to personal, lived experiences or to the invention of a culture."[33]

As Touraine notes, he himself contributed as much as he could to this demolition job. But all this does not mean

> that there is nothing between the strategy of head of state or the economic conjuncture and private life or writings, that the social situation is a network of tendencies and events and not the product of actions and social relations . . . A society which does not think itself can only sink into decadence, slowly or suddenly.[34]

While attacking those who attribute a spurious unity to either state or society, or who confuse the two, Touraine insists that "our role" as sociologists "is to rediscover the society behind the state, the social relation behind the role," and "to fight for society against the state."[35]

For the next ten years, Touraine worked solidly on the study of a variety of social movements, while restating his theoretical position in a number of articles, of which several are reproduced in *Le Retour de l'acteur* (1984). By now, the scene had shifted again; the post-modern challenge to any systematic theorizing about social relations and the new narcissism of post-public man coincided with a polarization of social theory between, on the one hand, a vision of society as a given order (a conception shared in different ways by Herbert Marcuse, Michel Foucault, Louis Althusser, Pierre Bourdieu and Erving Goffman – and, on the other, images taken from decision theory and organization theory. "*Society* splits apart: on the one side it is absorbed by state power; on the other it lags behind . . . cultural transformations, that is the construction of relations with the environment."[36]

In the face of what he calls again, as he had done in *La Société invisible*, an "anti-sociology,"[37] Touraine takes the current anxiety over the use of the words "social" or "society"[38] as a base from which to relaunch his own theoretical model. His book is not, he insists, polemical, but is written from a position "trapped between on the one hand a new individualism which has lost its illusions and, on the other, the degenerate and bureaucratic forms of old representations of social life."[39] Touraine argues, as Bourdieu had done in *Distinction*

(1979), that the public is more concerned by social and cultural issues than by the traditional themes of high politics, but these issues (TV, contraception, euthanasia or genetic engineering) have not yet found political expression. The role of the sociologist should be to help these new social actors to find themselves and to reiterate the importance of some basic social and historical questions: are we stagnating or moving into new forms of society and cultures?[40] The decline of the nation-state in the countries where it first developed has led many commentators to see contemporary social conflicts as wholly disaggregated. In fact, however, they are increasingly centered around a single theme: "the way in which society will use its own capacity to act on itself."[41]

Like many thinkers in the late twentieth century, Touraine increasingly oriented his thinking around the theme of modernity, most importantly in a major book, *Critique de la modernité*, which he sees as a radicalization of the analysis in his earlier works.[42] In its traditional form, the concept of modernity was associated with the rise of the bourgeoisie and of the nation-state, all lumped together in the concept of society.[43] We shall never recover the historical certainties of the founders of sociology, but we need to continue to pose some of the same questions about the relation between state and civil society and the unity or diversity of social movements[44] and their relation to new forms of subjectivity.[45]

The development of Touraine's thought which I have traced here could be paralleled by that of a number of social theorists in the second half of the twentieth century. Increasingly, I think, the development of formal models and the defense of positions of principle have given way to more concrete and situated accounts of social reality. It is no accident that two of Touraine's most recent books, *Can We Live Together?* (1997/2000) and *Comment sortir du libéralisme?* (1999), have been concerned with the reconstruction of conceptions of social solidarity which were central to the concerns of Durkheim and many of his contemporaries in the last *fin de siècle*, and more broadly with "the capacity of a society to act on itself, through its ideas, its conflicts, its hopes."[46]

As he puts it in his reply to commentaries on his work in 1996:

> What I term "society" is the concrete historico-geographic ensemble
> which combines a mode of functioning with certain processes of
> change. But, even if it is politically strong, the unity of that ensemble
> is merely illusory. Analysis must break down this semblance of unity
> and discover beneath it the cultural orientations, social conflicts,
> social movements and the institutional and organisational forms
> which correspond to a particular state of relations between historical
> actors.[47]

A recent book by two sociologists close to Touraine,[48] François Dubet
and Danilo Martuccelli, develops something like this program. The
title, *Dans quelle société vivons-nous?* suggests that the authors are not
confronting the more radically skeptical positions discussed earlier.
They do, however, trace what they call "the decline of the idea of
society" as previously conceived, based on a strong conception of
modernity, the idea of system, the centrality of work and the primacy
of the nation-state. All these elements have fragmented, in the crisis
of modernity as a grand narrative of progress, the shift from systems
and organizations to emergent effects, post-industrial forms of work
and the weakening of the identification with the nation-state.
"Institutions have become organisations . . . classes have become
strata."[49] If we still need a concept of society to make sense of these
transformations, as the authors believe we do, it can only be one
which takes account of these processes of fragmentation and abandons
the idea of a central principle of societal organization.[50] This recon-
structed idea of society will also be one which gives a greater importance to representations as a constitutive element:

> The idea of modern society aimed to describe a reality which was
> purported to be "substantive". Henceforth, it can only conceive
> itself, in the absence of any definitive articulation, in terms of its
> own investigation into itself, and with a growing awareness of the
> impossibility of arriving at a definitive answer.[51]

In a deliberately paradoxical formulation, the authors write: "our society is a disarticulated totality . . . [but] . . . it is the disarticulation which determines the representation of the totality."[52]

The bulk of the book traces the elements of this disarticulated totality in more detail. Classes and strata have multiplied and diversified; the links between stratification and domination have weakened. Issues of exclusion or "precarity" have become more prominent:[53] "the figures of the poor and of the unemployed person have replaced that of the worker forced to work on an assembly line as symbols of the "'social question'."[54] "The economy, which used to be the foundation of social cohesion, has become the very place where social exclusion is entrenched and produced."[55] Institutions such as school, family or religious community have become less influential. Thus, in terms of Lockwood's distinction, "The integration of society is no longer achieved by . . . a general coordination of conduct."[56] And yet:

> Social integration has undoubtedly lost its coherence and its clarity, but it is not certain that one should abandon the model . . . First, individual experience projected by deinstitutionalisation remains a social experience based in unequal social relations . . . Secondly, individuals seek to define themselves in collective identities and roots which they mobilise to construct their individuality, thus creating other types of social relations.[57]

Identities, they write, have become multiple and flexible. Social movements have proliferated. The self-representation of society takes place increasingly via the mass media. Politics, which used to provide a quasi-religious unity to society, has become fragmented and fluid in ways which reflect the increasingly complex and cross-cutting divisions within society. Yet all this means not the death of the idea of society, but merely that of "a central principle of its structuration."[58]

> The idea of society, to the extent that it does not flow "harmoniously", and above all directly, from classes or institutions, that is,

71

from social structures in the strong sense of the term, must hence-
forth be constructed in full awareness of its incompleteness and its
temporary character. If a new conception of modernity is bound up
with this transformation of our representation of the idea of society,
it now lies in the growing awareness of the aleatory character of
social representations.[59]

Dubet and Martuccelli stress that the classical idea of society involves
a particular conception of modernity and a particular social and
political philosophy.[60] Peter Wagner's work on modernity and the
social sciences converges on these themes and brings out a rather
sharper political reference. As Wagner points out, following Robert
von Mohl in the mid-nineteenth century, "society" emerges in the
eighteenth century and particularly since the French Revolution
into a conceptual family which, since the Renaissance in Europe,
had already two members and whose relations had been abundantly
theorized in liberal political philosophy; the individual and the state
or polity. At the time of Mohl's article (1851), Marx was not yet in
the picture, except as a political polemicist, but Adam Smith and the
other thinkers of the Scottish Enlightenment and, more recently,
Hegel and Tocqueville had addressed the emergent reality of society.

> All these thinkers' approaches have one feature in common . . . They
> all claim that major elements of the social world cannot, or can no
> longer, be grasped through the mere distinction between polity and
> household or, in the modern liberal form, between polity and
> individual. In this sense, these "sociologists" perform a break with an
> earlier representation of the moral-political on grounds, as they claim,
> of a transformed empirical reality. Doing so, however, they used the
> earlier representation as a resource with which to model the new
> one; i.e. they added one key element to an existing discourse rather
> than develop an entirely new representation. This choice . . . was
> motivated by the fact that these authors retained the interest in
> theorizing the form and feasibility of moral-political order that had
> informed both Greek and classical liberal thought. "Society" was
> investigated because of the change in political reasoning its existence

might require, not because, say, the production of pins or the asso-
ciative life in America was found intrinsically interesting.[61]

The question, then, became where society fitted in relation to its
two elder siblings, the polity or state and the individual. We have
already seen in Chapter 1 some of the main ways in which this has
been played out. There was a conservative reaction that the state could
do all the conceptual work required, and that the preoccupation
with society was at best unnecessary and at worst disloyal. Heinrich
von Treitschke, as Wagner shows, made this objection in 1859 in
direct response to Mohl. It recurs in 1908 in an unfavorable comment on Simmel by the Baden Minister of Culture: "It is, in my
opinion, a most perilous error to put 'society' in place of state and
church as the decisive [*massgebend*] organ of human coexistence."[62]
The radical alternative runs from Tom Paine's slogan that "society is
produced by our wants, and government by our wickedness,"[63]
through Marx and Engels' expectation that the state under communism would die away, to Pierre Clastres' nostalgia for society without
the state.[64] A more moderate sociological version makes the political
just one subsystem in a strongly integrated society and political sociology just one subdiscipline, along with the sociology of the family
or of sport. Wagner, with his eye both on "the coming into being
and the (almost) passing away of 'society'"[65] turns the tables on this
sociologistic conception:

> The sociological tradition tended to regard the social and socially
> determined nature of human life as one of its most important insights.
> Without entirely doing away with it, we should rather consider it as
> the question sociology contributed to social and political thought,
> not as the answer to all questions.[66]

For Wagner, then, society did not provide an answer to the political
problem which preceded it, that of the relation between individuals
and the political order. In the "second crisis of modernity," which is
a crisis of many of the social forms such as the work society and the

welfare state which had developed in response to the first, nineteenth-century crisis, processes of individualization, on the one hand, and globalization, on the other, have rendered strong conceptions of society even less plausible. Durkheimian society, one might say, is no more likely to solve our problems than the Hegelian state or a Marxian revolution. A more modest conception, however, owing less to Durkheim and more to Simmel and Max Weber, might be sustained.[67] We still need something of this kind, for two reasons. First, the political problem already noted. Second, because "none of the alternatives to the sociological mode or reasoning which are currently in vogue, and certainly not rationalist individualism, will be able to deal with what could more prudently be called the representation of the state of social relations."[68]

This last phrase can serve as the conclusion to this chapter. All the thinkers discussed here in fact agree, with varying degrees of emphasis, on the possibility and the importance of the representation of social relations. This might not seem surprising, were it not that thinkers as important as Hayek and Luhmann, not to mention the postmodernists, have questioned this possibility. Where Peter Wagner sees a return to broader concerns of social and political thought after the dominance of the sociological (including, of course, Marxist) way of understanding the relations between the social and the political, I would be inclined to locate this in a longer-term history in which they are always inseparably interrelated.

6

Towards a Synthesis?
Theory and metatheory

I have been siding, then, with the more cautious analyses of "society" in the late twentieth and early twenty-first centuries – with Bhaskar against Harré, with Touraine, Wagner or Freitag against Hayek or Baudrillard, with Martin Shaw against John Urry. Such differences between paradigms cannot be resolved by single arguments, but it is possible to suggest some ways in which the more moderate option can be made plausible. I should now like to sketch out a model which attempts to bring together metatheoretical and substantive theoretical considerations, and which can do justice to the multiplicity of social relations under conditions of advanced modernity.

Roy Bhaskar distinguished in *A Realist Theory of Science*[1] between three broad metatheoretical options which he called empirical realism, transcendental idealism and transcendental realism. Empirical realism postulates a correspondence between sensory experiences and the objects of those experiences; the objects of science are empirically given. Empirical realism equates the real with what has been or could be perceived: what you see is what you get.

This empirical realism is to be distinguished from what Bhaskar calls transcendental realism, which insists on the distinction between three domains: the real (underlying structures and mechanisms), the actual (events) and the empirical (observations). To be is neither just to happen nor just to be perceived. Some real processes, such as tooth

decay, may be perceptible only in their effects, and may be counteracted by other processes, such as teeth-brushing or the chemical
effects of fluoride. We are able to sit still to write or read because of
the interaction of two very powerful forces, the centrifugal effect of
the Earth's rotation and the countervailing force of its gravitational
attraction. For empirical realism, the ultimate object of science is the
"empirical world." For transcendental idealism, it is the theoretical
entities, models etc with which we attempt to capture the world
and to "save the phenomena," while for transcendental realism it is
the structures, mechanisms and processes of reality itself, the intrans-
itive objects of science which can be distinguished from its transitive
objects: our theories and concepts.

If we transfer these metatheoretical models of science to substantive social theory, we can map them onto the traditional theoretical
options in the conceptualization of society. Empirical realism offers
a stark choice. Either society is a holistic entity, on the analogy of a
biological organism, or "society" (in scare quotes) is a pre-scientific
and meaningless concept which is of no use in the study of particular
and necessarily individual social phenomena. For transcendental
idealism, society is an abstract principle of sociation (*Vergesellschaftung*),
often located in the perceptions of "its" members, as in Simmel's
brilliant social Kantianism in his excursus "How is Society Possible?".
For Simmel:[2]

> the unity of society needs no observer. It is directly realised by its
> own elements because these elements are themselves conscious and
> synthesising units . . . the consciousness of constituting with others a
> unity is actually all there is to this unity.

Here, the possibility of society becomes interwoven with the possibility of our knowledge of it – in other words, the possibility of
sociology.[3] This would, indeed, be one way of mitigating the apparent
idealism of Simmel's formulation, though it rather goes against
Simmel's statement that he is not putting forward a conception of
society as a "purely transcendental presupposition of sociological

experience."[4] In an interesting discussion of the relation between conceptions of society and the nation-state, Daniel Chernilo has followed this strategy, conceiving the role of "society" in sociology as that of a regulative idea:

> Different conceptions of society mediate between sociology's *theoretical tools* and *epochal diagnoses* in order to understand the social world of which sociology itself is a part. For the different periods of "classical", "modernist" and "cosmopolitan" sociology, . . . by looking at how the idea of society is defined, one can clarify the ways in which conceptual apparatuses (the canon) relate to epochal diagnoses and this is society's regulative role in the development of sociological thinking.[5]

More dramatically, in a materialist inversion of Simmel which recalls that performed at around the same time by Lukács, the Austro-Marxist Max Adler suggests that sociation under capitalist conditions is precisely an unconscious process, "in which all acts of sociation must merely be performed by isolated individuals who are not conscious of their sociation."[6] Simmel's *a priori*s seem in any case to be material as much as ideal; he presents them as "categories of reality" which are not merely tools in the hand of the social theorist but are constitutive of social interaction itself.[7]

One can usefully distinguish the theoretical constitution of, for example, "society" as an object in the mind of the sociologist from the practical constitution of society in human praxis, interaction, etc. Only the most extreme idealist or materialist would identify the two, seeing, respectively, human practice as ultimately nothing but the development of Mind/Spirit or cognitive practice as indistinguishable from other forms of practice. It is, however, easy to see *a priori* two possible mediations of these two concepts of constitution. In the first, the cognitive process is guided by the exigencies of practical intervention in the world. As Marx put it in the "Theses on Feuerbach," "all theoretical problems find their solution in practice." In a stronger version, following Vico,[8] the world may be said to be knowable to the extent that it is man-made. (This idea seems to be clearly present in Marx and parts of the Marxist tradition, and especially in Alfred Schmidt's work.[9]) In the second version, the constitution of reality in general or social reality in particular is to some degree a product of cognitive acts of constitution – interpretations, definitions of the situation, etc.

Simmel seems to equivocate between two questions:

1 How is society possible as an object of knowledge (for social theorists and other members of society)?
2 How is society possible as a practical accomplishment of its members?

If Simmel's answer to question (2) is taken to be "By acts of knowledge,"[10] the two questions collapse into one, yielding an idealist conception of the empirical genesis and foundation of society.[11] Alternatively, one can take Simmel (and *a fortiori* Max Adler) to be really asking "How is sociology possible?"; then, however, "sociology" must surely be understood in a more general sense than usual – as something like "intellectual representations of social relations." This would mesh in neatly with Simmel's insistence that the social *a prioris* are to be understood as constitutive "categories of reality" and not merely tools in the hand of the social theorist; it would also fit well with John O'Neill's phenomenological reading.[12]

In talking of a transcendental idealist conception of society, I do not, however, wish to confine this category to peripheral aspects of the thought of Simmel and Adler. What I have in mind is the more diffuse conception outlined in Chapter 1, which eschews the concept of society, preferring that of "sociation" and related categories of "process." And there is no doubt that this is a central theme of Simmel's work:

> one should properly speak, not of society, but of sociation. Society merely is the name for a number of individuals, connected by interaction . . . society certainly is not a "substance", nothing concrete, but an event: it is the function of receiving and affecting the fact and development of one individual by another.[13]

Earlier, in "Über sociale Differenzierung,"[14] Simmel had argued more aggressively that "society" is no more the object of sociology than "the cosmos" is the object of astronomy; the latter actually studies, for example, the movements of individual stars. Again, in *The Field of Sociology*, Simmel emphasizes that "Sociology . . . is founded upon an abstraction from concrete reality, performed under the guidance of the concept of society."[15]

Schrader-Klebert (see note 3) argues that Simmel's concept of society should be seen as a regulative idea in Kant's sense – "the hypothetical concept of the subject-matter [*Sache*] which is to arise successively in scientific cognition." This interpretation is certainly supported by the quotation above and by the following more inductivist formulation from a lecture given by Simmel in 1899:

> We cannot start from a concept of society, for society is the sum of the ways in which human beings act with or against one another. Only when we know all these ways will we have the concept of society. Definitions are valueless and empty.[16]

"Society," Simmel seems to believe, cannot be analyzed in a wholly positive manner as a substantive reality. Nor, however, can it simply be dissolved into individual scraps of social knowledge, since it is the abstract principle of society or social determination which constitutes these findings as social knowledge. The concept of society is not really transcendentally given, despite Simmel's references to Kant, but one which can be, in Schrader-Klebert's phrase, "reflexively recovered."[17] It is, however, legitimated not only by our cognitive interests but also by the nature of reality:

> Abstractions alone produce science out of the complexity or the unity of reality. Yet however urgently such abstractions may be demanded by the needs of cognition itself, they also require some sort of justification of their relation to the structure of the objective world. For only some functional relation to actuality can save one from sterile inquiries or from the haphazard formulation of scientific concepts.[18]

Max Weber, as we saw earlier, does not attempt to give his sociology any transcendental foundation. His (negative) concept of society, however, has a considerable affinity with Simmel's. We have already noted the consistently hostile attitude to the abuse of holistic concepts which Weber displayed in a letter to Robert Liefmann:

> If I have become a sociologist (according to my letter of accreditation), it is mainly in order to exorcise the spectre of collective conceptions which still lingers among us. In other words, sociology itself can only proceed from the actions of one or more separate individuals and must therefore adopt strictly individualistic methods.[19]

Weber, as we saw, scarcely ever uses the word "society" (except, of course, in the title of his principal work); it seems clear that he associated the term with spuriously scientific sociologies which treat society as a substantial entity. *Gemeinschaft* appears rather more frequently, and does not seem to raise the same anxieties in Weber. In the case of both terms, however, he generally uses the processual forms *Vergemeinschaftung* and *Vergesellschaftung*; this is, of course, in keeping with Tönnies's own ideal-typical formulation of the antithesis: "I do not know of any condition of culture and society in which elements of *Gemeinschaft* and elements of *Gesellschaft* are not simultaneously present, that is, mixed."[20]

Weber's more general strategy of reducing social structural phenomena to complexes of action goes along with this relatively abstract and "negative" concept of society. With Simmel, the influences seem to be of a more general philosophical kind, while Tönnies was strongly influenced by Schopenhauer's concept of the will.[21]

What I am calling here, in an informal sense, transcendental idealist concepts of society were carried further in interactionist and "phenomenological" sociology. The US interactionist, Herbert Blumer, for example, put it in these terms: "The human being is not swept along as a neutral and indifferent unit by the operation of a system . . . cultural norms, status positions and role relationships are only frameworks inside of which [the] process of formative transaction goes on."[22] In 1932, Alfred Schutz, the father of phenomenological sociology, cited with approval Simmel's "underlying idea . . . that all concrete social phenomena should be traced back to the modes of individual behaviour."[23] The same idea is developed in Berger and Luckmann's classic book, *The Social Construction of Reality*, discussed in more detail in Chapter 2:

> The central question for sociological theory can . . . be put as follows: How is it possible that subjective meanings *become* objective facticities . . . In other words, an adequate understanding of the "reality *sui generis*" of society requires an inquiry into the manner in which this reality is constructed.[24]

The theme of "reality construction" was of course pushed to an extreme in the sociology of the later twentieth century, and has enjoyed a further wave with the (rather slow) sociological reception of postmodernism discussed in Chapter 3. There is, however, another current, linked to the names of the Austro-Marxist, Max Adler, and the neo-Marxist, Theodor Adorno, in which a transcendental idealist concept of society shifts towards what I would call a transcendental realist conception. The two salient features of this process are, first, a stronger emphasis on social determination and, second, an awareness of the extra-theoretical origins and political significance of the concept of society, taken up later by Peter Wagner.

Max Adler, as we have seen, closely followed Simmel in demanding an epistemological foundation for sociology. However, the works in which he developed this theme should be seen in the context of his keen awareness of the historical development of the concept of society. Adler notes that Marx, in *The Holy Family*, recognizes the illusory and ideological nature of the image of society as made up of isolated individuals. Like Hegel,

> [Marx] takes as the starting-point of [his] sociological treatment of the problem of society the conception of bourgeois society as a mere appearance of the atomistic independence of its elements . . . In Marx,

this appearance is shown to be the necessary product of a particular historical form of human sociation, namely the form in which all acts of sociation must merely be performed by isolated individuals who are not conscious of their sociation, a form which is overcome by the removal of this social order.[25]

This sense of the problematic nature of sociation in bourgeois society is developed further by Adorno. The sense in which Adorno uses the term "society" in the singular, what he calls an "emphatic"concept of society, denotes "the moment of sociation . . . i.e. that there exists between human beings a functional connection . . . which takes on a certain kind of independence in relation to them."[26] "Noch die biographische Einzelperson ist eine soziale Kategorie." Even the individual is a social category.[27]

Adorno's concept of society is in some respects very close to Simmel's. Both see sociation as a functional relation or what Adorno calls a "category of mediation."[28] The affirmation of society does not mean a depreciation of the individual, though it does involve an emphasis that individuals are constituted by society and, like all other social phenomena, can only be understood in relation to the social totality. Hence Adorno's hostility to those, whether empirical researchers or theorists, who dispense with the concept of society:

> It is on account of this functional structure that the notion of society cannot be grasped in any immediate fashion, nor is it susceptible of drastic verification, as are laws of the natural sciences. Positivistic currents in sociology tend therefore to dismiss it as a mere philosophical survival. Yet such realism is itself unrealistic. For while the notion of society may not be deduced from any individual facts, nor on the other hand be apprehended as an individual fact itself, there is nonetheless no social fact which is not determined by society as a whole. Society appears as a whole behind each concrete social situation.[29]

In a characteristically Marxian turn, Adorno argues that the abstraction implicit in the concept of society is not a matter of the sociological theorist's banal reflection that "everything is connected with everything else" – rather, it is the essence of the exchange process which is fundamental to society in the modern sense.[30] More ambitiously still, he argues that there is a conceptuality (*Begrifflichkeit*) in social relations themselves, most notably in the exchange relation:

> It is futile to ask whether . . . [such] . . . essential connections are "real", or merely conceptual structures. The person who attributes the conceptual to social reality need not fear the accusation of being idealistic. What is implied here is not merely the constitutive conceptuality of the knowing subject but also a conceptuality which holds sway in reality [*Sache*] itself.
>
> Exchange value, merely a mental configuration when compared with use value, dominates human needs and replaces them; illusion dominates reality. To this extent, society is myth and its elucidation is still as necessary as ever. At the same time, however, this illusion is what is most real, it is the formula used to bewitch the world.[31]

This theme of the interpenetration of thought and reality is central to Adorno's concept of society (as it is to his thought in general). What he does, in essence, is to restore the polemical edge which the concept had in the bourgeois revolutions of the eighteenth and nineteenth centuries and in the liberal problematic of "the individual" versus "society" or "the state." Adorno has a more Marxist and Freudian concept of the individual, but he restores the pathos of the original discussion, believing that reification and social control are now immeasurably stronger:

> The more the subjects are grasped by society, and . . . the more completely they are determined by the system, the more the system maintains itself not simply by the use of force against the subjects, but also through the subjects themselves.[32]

This theme is brought out in more concrete terms in Adorno's discussion of the relationship between sociology and psychology.[33] The susceptibility of "the masses" to irrational appeals, in particular those of fascism, requires psychological analysis as well as a sociological investigation of mass movements: "For the masses would hardly succumb to the brazen wink of untrue propaganda if something within them did not respond to the rhetoric of sacrifice and the dangerous life."[34] Thus, the relationship between sociology and psychology has been fundamentally misconceived where it is seen only in terms of the classification of the sciences or their multi-disciplinary integration:

> Where any thought at all has been devoted to the relation between social theory and psychology, it has not gone beyond merely assigning the two disciplines their place within the total scheme of the sciences: the difficulties their relation involves have been treated as a matter of employing the right conceptual model. Whether social phenomena are to be derived from objective conditions or from the psyche of socialised individuals, or from both: whether the two types of explanation complete or exclude one another, or whether their relationship itself requires further theoretical consideration – all this is reduced to mere methodology.
>
> The way social and individual, objective and psychic, moments relate to one another is supposedly dependent on the mere conceptual schematisation imposed on them in the busy academic process; plus the usual reservation that a synthesis would at this stage be premature, that more facts have to be gathered and concepts more sharply defined.[35]

Thus, although "all varieties of psychologism that simply take the individual as their point of departure are ideological,"[36]

> a psychology that turns its back on society and idiosyncratically concentrates on the individual and his archaic heritage says more about the hapless state of society than one which seeks by its "wholistic approach" or an inclusion of social "factors" to join the ranks of a no longer existent *universitas literarum*.[37]

> the difference between individual and society is not merely quantitative, and it is seen this way only from the blinkered perspective of a social process that from the outset moulds the individual into a mere

84

agent of his function in the total process. No future synthesis of the social sciences can unite what is inherently at odds with itself.[38]

Adorno develops a similar argument in relation to the theories of Weber and Durkheim. Weber's stress on the "understanding" of social phenomena and Durkheim's insistence that they should be treated as things are equally one-sided and partial.[39] Each must be understood both in respect of its partial justification and as an expression of a "false" state of society. An atomistic, individualizing sociology reflects an atomized and administered society;[40] Durkheim's opposite stress on social constraint expresses, but does not analyse, the reification to which such a society is also prone.[41] Taken together, they demonstrate in a quite open and unpretentious manner the need for a dialectical theory of society which does justice to both these contradictory moments.[42]

What would such a theory look like in practice? Adorno is notoriously long on critique and short on positive statements; indeed, one of his central claims is that the latter must be treated with suspicion as sources of reification. For all this, however, a clear and powerful account can be found in his writings. His concept of society is intimately linked to his account of the relation between theory and data – something with which Adorno is not generally associated. As we have seen, "society" is a theoretical concept *par excellence*: "Because society can neither be defined as a concept in the current logical sense, nor empirically demonstrated, while in the meantime social phenomena continue to call out for some kind of conceptualization, the proper organ of the latter is speculative theory."[43] Such theorizing is not to be seen as an alternative to empirical research, but as complementary, though relatively autonomous. The important distinction is not between theory and research, but between research which is conducted with an eye to the social totality and that which deliberately brackets out any such "speculative" reference. The former was essentially the approach of the Institute for Social Research. Adorno argued, for example, that the analysis of class conflicts must seek them out in areas remote from the visible conflict between capital and labor in, for example, interpersonal relationships and in the psychological domain.[44] Similarly, one of the main themes of his work in the sociology of music was, of course, to elucidate the effects in this domain of the exchange relation, reification and fetishism.[45] The principle is the same throughout; however specific the theme of a particular investigation, sociology should be concerned with "the essential laws of society, [which] are not what the richest possible empirical findings have in common."[46] As Adorno put it in an autobiographical essay:

> Whether one proceeds from a theory of society and interprets the allegedly reliably observed data as mere epiphenomena upon the theory, or, alternatively, regards the data as the essence of science and the theory of society as a mere abstraction derived from the ordering of the data – these alternatives have far-reaching substantial consequences for the conception of society. More than any specific bias or "value judgement", the choice of one or the other of these frames of reference determines whether one regards the abstraction "society" as the most fundamental reality, controlling all particulars, or on account of its abstractness considers it, in the tradition of nominalism, as a mere *flatus vocis*. These alternatives extend into all social judgements, including the political.[47]

I have suggested that what one finds in Adorno is a transcendental idealist concept of society, similar to Simmel's, but one which is fundamentally transformed in a realist direction by being located in a materialist theory – a theory which is more reflexive than, or reflexive in a different way from, that of Simmel. Here, I suggest, we can see the point at which a transcendental idealist model of society as a regulative idea for its members and, by extension, for the sociologist, turns into a transcendental realist model of society as an imperceptible yet nonetheless real structure determining, in the sense of shaping, concrete human actions.

What might such a model look like? Roy Bhaskar has offered not just the metatheoretical framework which I have been using in this chapter but also a sketch of a realist theory of society which can usefully be compared with other recent works dealing with the relation between action and structure.[48] First, we need to ask just what conception of society a realist theory might be committed to. I suggest that the essential principle of such a theory is the reality of structures and of the relations within and between structures (in particular, causal relations).[49] In other words, it is required of whatever social structures and mechanisms are postulated that they be in some sense real, rather than heuristic devices, and that they explain satisfactorily (without being reducible to) the observable phenomena of social life.

This is, I think, enough to distinguish a realist conception of society or social structure from empirical realist or transcendental idealist ones. What constraints does it set, though, on candidates for social structural mechanisms? In principle, none. The realist distinction between the real and the empirical is precisely designed to legitimate the postulation of entities which are observable only via their effects, for which they provide the best available explanation in terms of current theory.[50] As we saw in Chapter 2, Rom Harré can frame what he would see as realist explanations in terms of discursive structures and practices. In other words, although both Harré and Bhaskar uphold a relational ontology of the social, their ontologies are radically different.[51] Bhaskar adopts the strategy of a "pincer movement."[52] Society is not reducible to people and their actions, since it is a condition of those actions. At the same time, society does not exist independently of individuals and their actions.[53] We are therefore back with Berger and Luckmann's question: "How is it possible that human activity [*Handeln*] should produce a world of things [*choses*]?"[54] But this question is badly posed; what is at issue is not the Robinsonian creation of social structures which then reform the individuals who created them. To put the matter in this way "encourages, on the one hand, a voluntaristic idealism with respect to our understanding of social structure and, on the other, a mechanistic determinism with respect to our understanding of people."[55] People do not create society, but reproduce or transform it: "Society is both the ever-present *condition* (material cause) and the continually

87

reproduced *outcome* of human agency."[56] "Society stands to individuals, then, as something that they never make, but that exists only in virtue of their activity."[57]

It should be stressed that Bhaskar's use of the term "society" is deliberately open in these formulations, and therefore neutral in relation to some of the oppositions with which we have been concerned here. Social structures or societies, in this model, are both activity-dependent and concept-dependent. This is a relational conception of the social which opposes attempts to ground it in individuals, groups (with society being seen as a sort of super-group), masses or whatever.[58] The connections between action and structure are made, in large part, through "positions" and "practices" which are specified relationally. One advantage of the relational conception, Bhaskar suggests, is that

> It allows one to focus on a range of questions, having to do with the *distribution* of the structural conditions of action, and in particular with differential allocations of: (i) productive resources (of all kinds, including for example cognitive resources) to persons (and groups) and (ii) persons (and groups) to functions and roles (for example in the division of labour).[59]

Here there is a close parallel with two other major theoretical projects: Anthony Giddens' structuration theory and Margaret Archer's alternative conception of morphogenesis, which has origins in, and remains tied to, a sophisticated version of system theory and which she has come to frame in terms of a realist metatheory. Giddens' theory of structuration, most fully presented in *The Constitution of Society*, is based on the idea that the dualism "between subject and social object" or, as it has come to be expressed, between agency and structure

> has to be reconceptualized as a duality – the duality of structure . . .

> The structural properties of social systems exist only in so far as forms of social conduct are reproduced chronically across time and space.[60]

Except in the title of his book, Giddens tends to put the terms "society" and "societies" in scare quotes:

> We have to be very careful with the concept of "social system" and the associated notion of "society". They sound innocent terms, and they are probably indispensable if used with appropriate measures of caution. "Society" has a useful double meaning . . . – signifying a bounded system, and social association in general . . .
> Functionalism and naturalism tend to encourage unthinking acceptance of societies as clearly delimited entities, and social systems as internally highly integrated entities. For such perspectives . . . tend to be closely allied to biological concepts; and these have usually been arrived at with reference to entities clearly set off from the world around them. But "societies" are very often not like this at all.[61]

Archer agrees with Giddens that the relation between structure and agency is not one between macro and micro, the large-scale and the small:

> the central theoretical task is one of linking two *qualitatively* different aspects of society, (the "social" and the "systemic", or if preferred, "action" and its "environment") rather than two quantitatively different features, the big and the small or macro and micro.[62]

For her, however, Giddens' concept of stucturation is too undifferentiated, conflating the two levels of action and structure or system rather than holding them apart analytically in the manner of Lockwood's distinction between system integration and social integration. The distinctiveness of the system level is marked, in particular, by its temporal dimension. The demographic structure of a population, for example, although of course it is sustained by individual reproductive behavior, deaths, etc., is not amenable to immediate change. When President de Gaulle, in one of France's regular natalist campaigns, asked the French people to produce "twelve million beautiful babies," he knew that this could not happen overnight. Rather than thinking of structures and systems just as in an ongoing manner reproduced by action, we should focus more on the way in which they precede action and are modified by it, in a process she calls structural elaboration, taking the form of morphogenesis, the modification of forms, or morphostasis, their preservation.[63]

This undoubtedly is a valid point, but I am less sure that it sustains the move into system theory, with its attendant attempt to draw clear-cut analytical distinctions between, for example, structure and culture. This is not just a matter of their constant interrelation, which of course Archer accepts.[64] It is more that I am less sure that it is possible to draw even a clear analytical distinction between them. There is a difference, in other words, between using such concepts in a cautious and tentative manner, as I think Archer does in her substantive work, and postulating their existence, albeit provisionally, in the strong terms to which realism is committed.[65]

I believe, in other words, that the system route is not the way to construct a defensible concept of society. On the other hand, I strongly agree with Archer that a realist metatheory resolves many of the traditional dilemmas in the opposition between individualism and collectivism[66] and that the convergence between Bhaskar's "philosophical critique of the contemporary human sciences"[67] and some of the most interesting contemporary sociological writing on the relations of action and structure, and related issues of ideology and critique, is an exceptionally important achievement of the social theory of the late twentieth century.[68]

What does a realist metatheory imply for social theory, and particularly for theorizing about society? As I have argued elsewhere, it is a mistake to tie a realist metatheory to specific theoretical options, though the realist emphasis on the stratification of reality at least discourages certain forms of reductionism and certain empiricist moves which have influenced (or more bluntly discouraged) social theorizing. To examine the large range of explicitly realist recent contributions to social theory would take us too far from the focus of this book, but it is worth noting in particular the work of Andrew Sayer,[69] as well as a number of contributions to the two Routledge series in critical realism.[70]

What I have been arguing for, then, is a realist philosophy of science and a realist ontology of the social. This ontology views society as both a condition and a continuously reproduced outcome of action. What is provided here is a real definition of society, i.e. a definition which makes truth-functional claims about reality. Such a definition is therefore distinct from ordinary usage, in the sense that it may involve abstract theoretical concepts, and yet is likely at the same time to be linked in complex ways to our contemporary and historical experience of sociality. W.I. Thomas's dictum that "if men [*sic* people] define things as real, they are real in their consequences" holds in a negative sense too. A society which does not think of itself in terms of society, like a class which does not think of itself in class terms, is likely to behave in rather different ways from one which does.[71] In particular, of course, they are less likely to develop forms and practices of solidarity. But all this is still sociation, which must be related to some conception of a social totality, even if its boundaries are indistinct.

How might one link up these relatively abstract reflections to society as an object of and, for some at least, a context for reflection in the early twenty-first century? A recent collection of interviews edited by Nicholas Gane, *The Future of Social Theory*, provides an interesting snapshot of current approaches to the concepts of society and the social on the part of some leading theorists. Gane formulates in the Introduction one of the main questions he explores:

> Could it be that "society" (which tended to be theorized as being contained within the territorial limits of the nation-state) is all but dead, or is it possible that (capitalist) society is recasting itself in new global, post-national directions? Or might it be that the social itself is no longer confined (if it ever was) within the limits of society or the nation-state, and is increasingly fluid and diverse in form?[72]

At the skeptical end of the spectrum of responses, Zygmunt Bauman, in a chapter entitled "Liquid Sociality," restates the position examined in Chapter 3, in this volume. He contrasts the emphasis on adaptation to fixed circumstances characteristic both of the social psychology of the 1950s and of his own life-experience with the fluidity of the contemporary world.[73] He returns to his well-known gardening metaphor:

> at no stage in their lives can individuals be correctly described as "embedded" (even if only temporarily and "until further notice") because flowerbeds have ceased to be as clearly defined as before; their boundaries are now unclear if not washed out altogether. Instead of seeking their proper, prefabricated locations, individuals must conjure up the locations as they go – and the only roads in sight are the lines of footprints they have left behind. Society no longer looks like a garden; it seems to have returned to a wilderness, or rather a secondary wilderness, a frontier-land, where locations need to be first carved and fenced off to be fit for settlement.[74]

John Urry, too, restates his critique of the way conceptions of society have been tied to the nation-state:

> I am not saying that somehow societies or nation-states have now simply disappeared. That would obviously be false. But that something of this tying together, this sort of connectivity, of society with nation-state, has come to be significantly weakened . . . Yet much sociological work still takes "society" for granted and presumes by this that there is an integrated nation-state society.[75]

From a rather different focus, that of the social as an object of social policy and governance, Nikolas Rose addresses some exceptionally interesting issues concerning the concept of society. At the time when Jacques Donzelot was writing *The Policing of Families* (1977) and the still untranslated *L'invention du social* (1984):[76]

> many intellectuals and politicians were already beginning to question the inevitability of the belief that individuals were determined and shaped by society, that individual rights had to be subordinated to social obligations, and that insurance against risk was best secured by schemes of social provision, and so forth . . . People still refer to

society, of course; they have not simply erased that reference to all the forces and processes that bind human beings together beyond their individuality and their family relations. But the social vocabulary for accounting for these does not have a monopoly any more, with terms like community, for example, being the most common substitute these days for the idea of the social.[77]

Clearly, from the point of view of sociologists who want to explore the networks of relations that exist between human beings in certain times and spaces, "societies" still exist as loose frameworks for defining the object of study, though even here the concept imposes rather too much unity upon these frameworks. But "society," in the way sociologists such as Durkheim thought about it, no longer exists. For a hundred years, sociologists and others thought about societies as almost natural in kind – discrete, bounded and territorialized (usually by the nation-state) – with their own kind of relatively uniform culture, mores, family forms, patterns of socialization, and so forth. This idea of society is hardly sustainable today, conceptually or empirically.[78]

Rose puts the issue very well, I think, though in slightly starker terms than I would wish to. First, the traditional concept of society which he describes was much less strong in German and much British and North American social thought than in France, where the Durkheimian influence was dominant. Second, the eclipse of the notion of society is perhaps not as striking or uniform as Rose suggests, especially if one counts current discussion of "community" as covering something like the same notions, outside the seminar rooms where they are, hopefully, more clearly differentiated.

The French sociologist or, as he prefers to consider himself, anthropologist, Bruno Latour takes much the same line, in more aggressive language,[79] while offering a way out in the form of an alternative concept of association:

> there were already at the origin of sociology, at least in France, two traditions. One of them saw the social as a special part of reality, different from geology, biology, economics and so on, and another one saw very well that what counts in the social is the type of connections

that are made. In this view, the social is not a homogeneous domain of reality composed of social elements, but a movement between non-social elements – a piece of law, a laboratory practice, etc. – connected in certain ways.[80]

On this account, as we saw earlier, the objection to "society" is that it is a cheap and lazy way of pre-empting the detailed investigation of the empirically given connections.[81]

This potentially very fruitful suggestion that the concept of society be refigured in terms of association, and in particular the association of social and natural elements, is grounded in Latour's own work and that of his collaborators, and it also has resonances in several of the other interviews, notably that with John Urry discussed earlier and those with Scott Lash and Saskia Sassen. Metatheoretically and methodologically, too, it is interesting to note that several contributors to the volume refer to complexity theory, autopoiesis and self-organization (Ilya Prigogine, Isabelle Stengers, etc.) and other families of theories bridging the natural/social divide. (A further dimension, not really represented in this collection despite Lash's references to vitalism, but stressed by other social theorists such as Ted Benton, is the connection to biological reality.[82])

It is, however, only with Beck's contribution to the volume that we find, I think, a fundamental attempt to retain and reconstruct a defensible concept of society. It was Beck, of course, who introduced and popularized the concepts of risk society and world risk society and stressed the individualization of social positions in what he and others call second modernity. In his more recent work, he has addressed the issues of globalization and cosmopolitanism, seen in contrast to the "methodological nationalism" of previous social science, in an exceptionally innovative way. I shall discuss this in more detail in the following chapter, but for the moment it is sufficient to record as a marker his reflections on the concept of society:

I don't think we can substitute for society a concept of culture or of civilization, or . . . of network. Classical sociology conceptualized

94

society in a very sophisticated way. It used all kinds of different ideas to define society and to give it an important perspective in relation to the economy and politics . . .

economics, political science and cultural studies all fail to grasp what is new about the processes of globalization and cosmopolitanism. For what is new about these processes is the redefinition of society: *thinking society anew is the issue* . . .

society can and should be a concept which integrates many different elements: culture, politics, values, religion, technological developments, global risk dynamics, and so on . . .

Questions of redefinition and renegotiation . . . should concentrate on the concept of society.[83]

It is time to draw together the threads of this chapter. I have suggested that what I called, following Bhaskar, empirical realist conceptions of society either as a single quasi-organism or as merely collapsed into a collocation of isolated facts and/or individuals are not defensible. Society is the product of sociation, the actions of individuals in structured contexts. Strong neo-Kantian or social constructionist accounts which see sociation only in cognitive terms, however, do not do justice to the constraining and enabling power of social relations. In the last few sentences I have referred to society where I could have referred in a less ambitious way to social structures, which might be merely the act-action structures of Harré's interactionist and discursive model. But we need also to recognize the importance of processes of structuration at a societal level, where this may mean the traditional nationally inflected conception or something both more fragmented in its composition and more far-reaching in its scope. It is these processes of intensive and extensive multiplicity which are addressed most fully, perhaps, by Dubet and Martuccelli in the former case and by Beck in both,[84] but more substantially in the latter.

There remains, in other words, the substantive issue of how far sociation in this very broad sense takes place at what we might conventionally term a societal level and how far at other levels and through more indirect processes of influence and transmission (Urry's flows). Legal norms and directives might be a good example. Tradi-tionally emanating from the national state, they are now increasingly shaped by supranational processes and the interaction between lower-level and supranational bodies, as well as to some extent by world public opinion. Globalization and Europeanization, to anticipate the discussion in the final chapter, interact with localization and nation-alization, in what Adrienne Héritier has called a logic of diversity. Here Martin Shaw's metaphor of layers of state (sub-regional, national, supra-national or global) can be extended to what we might call layers of society. To take an example from a more informal area of social life, dress styles for young people may be shaped at a global and European level, yet also noticeably different in Flanders and Wallonia. I suggest in Chapter 8 that one can find at least elements of a European society and civil society which is distinct from those to be found (at regional or national level) in individual member states. Before addressing the question of the existence of something that might be called a European society, it may be useful to look at the concept of civil society which has been particularly prominent, both in discussions of Europe and, more generally, in social theory.

PART III
Implications

7

Society Lite?

Theories of civil society

As I have noted from time to time throughout this book, the eclipse of the concept of society has gone along with an uncritical adoption of alternative concepts. Chief among these is "community," where this is seen as somehow both more substantial and more attractive than "society." There are echoes of this also in the slightly more precise, though still quite diverse, use of the term "civil society" in the late twentieth and early twenty-first centuries.

As it happens, the two concepts, community and civil society, have a common origin in the late medieval and early modern reception of Aristotle's thought. What became the definitive Latin translation in the early fifteenth century used the term *societas civilis* for Aristotle's *koinonia politike* in place of terms such as *communitas* and *communio* which had been used earlier.[1] Hence, as Maurizio Viroli puts it, "*politeia*-related words were replaced by *civitas*-related words."[2]

This is not the place to speculate about the consequences of this shift for social and political theory, or to trace the subsequent history of the term which has been very fully documented in the massive study by Jean Cohen and Andrew Arato and by John Keane and others.[3] Very briefly, after a long period in which, even if it lexically seemed to suggest society rather than the state, in practice the term referred to the political sphere, it came to be used in English (and Scottish) political economy and philosophy to refer to a non-state

99

sphere of society, including both market and non-market transactions and related forms of association between "possessive" individuals. Hegel conceived of civil society, *bürgerliche Gesellschaft*, in this sense as an intermediate and egoistic sphere between the intimacy of the family and the rational and public-spirited universality of the state. For Marx, this reconciliation of antagonisms in the state is a pseudo-religious illusion: so-called civil society is bourgeois society (both, of course, *bürgerlich* in German) and the bourgeois state is not the expression of the universal interest of the members of society but an instrument of the class rule of the exploiting bourgeoisie. Despite its extremely creative use in the 1920s by the Italian Marxist, Antonio Gramsci, reflecting on the different structures of political opportunity in Italy compared to Russia, the concept fell out of use in the twentieth century, partly displaced by theories of mass society and mass politics.[4]

A century after Marx's death, when the Soviet Marxist-Leninist dictatorship was half a century old and the people's democracies which it had imposed on Eastern and central Europe had been in power for a quarter of a century, the term civil society experienced a double rehabilitation: in the East by anti-regime thinkers and activists, and in the West by neo-Marxists and other radicals reflecting both on the Eastern tyrannies and on the recent Western experience of 1968 and the rise of new social movements. Nor was this only, by any means, a European phenomenon; in authoritarian Brazil, wrote Fernando Cardoso: "everything which was an organized fragment was being designated *civil society*. Not rigorously, but effectively, the whole opposition . . . was being described as if it were the movement of Civil Society."[5]

For the Polish dissident Adam Michnik, reflecting on the experience of the 1980s, the idea was that communist power would be rolled back by civil society in a convergence of self-management and society independent from the state: "we invented something like alternative society, which would fulfil a substantial part of its needs independently from a totalitarian state."[6] As Krishan Kumar puts it in his book on 1989:

The failure of revolution (Hungary 1956) and reform from above (Czechoslovakia 1968) led to the idea of a third way: reform from below, by the construction or reconstruction of civil society. The Polish experience of the 1980s seemed to confirm the validity of this strategy.[7]

For a brief time in late 1989 and early 1990, it seemed, indeed, that civil society was on the brink of coming to power in Eastern Europe,[8] taking further the impetus of the Western social movements which by then had rather run out of steam.

By early 1990 it was clear that civil society was not coming to power, even in the more comfortable parts of the post-communist world, as established or newly created political parties consolidated their dominance. The concept of civil society in turn came in for a good deal of critical scrutiny. There was an understandable reaction against the inflationary use of the term in the early 1990s, associated with unrealistic expectations about post-communist transition. Civil society movements did not live up to the expectation that they would offer a new, higher form of democracy in part at least of the post-communist world; instead, they were rapidly elbowed out by new, reconstituted or reinvented political movements and institutions. In Ferenc Miszlivetz's classic formulation, "We dreamed of civil society and we got NGOs."[9] As Jadwiga Staniszkis concluded as early as 1991:

> the creation of a civil society is a much more complex process than mere political liberalization: it demands both property rights reform and deep cultural change. It is painful, just as is the creation of new politics occurring now in the Eastern bloc.[10]

The 1990s saw the triumph of economically and politically deterministic models of post-communist development at the expense of more socially and culturally oriented ones. Ralf Dahrendorf, in 1990, drew the classic distinction between the "hour of the (constitutional) lawyers," its immediate successor or accompaniment, "the hour of the politicians," and the much later "hour of the citizen."[11]

Dahrendorf's prediction of 60 years for the completion of civil society is of course a high estimate, but the general analysis now seems prophetic. Martin Krygier drew the same sort of conclusion somewhat later in the process: "Civil societies depend upon distinctive configurations of economic life, civility among acquaintances and strangers, and tolerant pluralism. These in turn depend upon particular configurations of state and law, and gain support from particular sorts of politics.[12]

What in fact happened in post-communist Europe was, broadly speaking, the adoption of political and economic fixes which were at least meant to be quick, with the social left to fend for itself insofar as it was not understood as merely the object of administrative "social" policy. For all the talk of civil society, in practice, it, and society as a whole, was largely forgotten. Disappointments of this kind, together with others about the fate of Western civil society movements, led to a revision of some of the implications of civil society thinking, pointing critically to its over-moralization into "neat" models which exclude anything distasteful. A useful collection of papers from a conference in 1998, for example, defines civil society in terms of "self-organization," presupposing "corresponding resources such as trust, communication skills and education" and "the recognition of diversity and the legitimacy of regulated conflict."[13] But while something like this may be a requirement for a functioning civil society as a whole, it should clearly, I think, not be automatically imputed to individual components of civil society. Neo-Nazi groups which are authoritarian and intolerant both in their public activities and in their internal organization are no less components of civil society, as I understand the term, than the more attractive and friendly movements which students of social movements have tended to concentrate on.

Those who object to the normative inflation of the concept of civil society have also often pointed to its possibly illiberal uses in certain contexts. Robert Fine illustrated some of these, notably in relation to South Africa.[14] More recently, Graham Pollock has argued, like Fine, that civil society theory has been constructed in opposition to a somewhat caricatured negative image of nationalism and national identity and sometimes acted as an ideological support to what he calls "banal state nationalism" such as that displayed by much of the Spanish political class in its backlash against Catalan and Basque nationalism.[15]

It is easy to retort that partisans of civil society have rather little to offer in the way of political murder, war, deportations and genocide compared to champions of the nation or *Volk* and the state, but some contemporary uses of civil society theory should give pause for thought. Despite all this, however, I continue to think both that we require some concept of civil society and that civil society politics in both its Western and Eastern European forms from the 1970s onwards remains one of our most fruitful political experiences and resources. What we need, I think, is a model of civil society which is critical but not moralistic, avoiding setting the entry costs too high while being more than a mere descriptive category of public administrative discourse, as it has tended to be for the EU and for some national governments, especially in post-communist Europe.[16]

Conceptions of civil society can be roughly divided into broader and narrower understandings of the term; Victor Pérez-Días (1998) distinguishes between "generalists" and "minimalists."[17] In the former conception, as for example in the quotations above from Staniszkis and Krygier and in Larry Siedentop's book, *Democracy in Europe*, it is principally conceived as a form of *society*, characterized by, *inter alia*, individualism, the rule of law, some sort of public sphere, and so forth:

> For what is fundamental to the idea of a civil society? It is that the equality of status attributed by states to their subjects creates, at least potentially, a sphere of individual liberty or choice, a private sphere of action.[18]

In the latter, narrower understanding of the term, it is presented as a form of *associational life* independent of the state and economy, the base of a pyramid, as it were, whose apex is formed by public

103

intellectuals and commentators and social movement activists. Whereas Pérez-Días favors a broader understanding of the term, Jeff Alexander has argued for many years for a more restricted one. My preference is for a weaker version of Alexander's usage, in which civil society is taken to mean associational life at a variety of levels, shading off into conceptions of the public sphere.[19] I would, however, be less restrictive than Alexander in that I would include low-level economic exchanges, especially in a post-communist context in which emergent market relations of a kind excluded under the communist regimes have been an important aspect of the building up of social ties. More importantly, though, there is a clear interrelation between the two conceptions, not just in the obvious sense that some degree of pluralism is necessary for autonomous associational life to be possible at all, but in more subtle ways in which the associations between component parts of a society influence the society and state as a whole. In John Keane's model of civil society, for example:

> [it] both describes and envisages a complex and dynamic ensemble of legally-protected non-governmental institutions that tend to be non-violent, self-organizing, self-reflexive, and permanently in tension with each other and with the state institutions that "frame", constrict and enable their activities.[20]

This is not a strong relation of entailment, however, since one can also point to situations in which there are independent intermediary institutions but nothing that one could call a civil society.[21] Authoritarian, as opposed to totalitarian, regimes would be one example, but another might be the case of the EU discussed in the following chapter. Here there is quite a bit of associational activity at a European level, but many observers would deny the existence of a civil society. Conversely, there may be a kind of civil society even where associational life is severely restricted, or where what civil society or public sphere that exists is controlled and monitored by the state.[22]

The post-communist context is of particular interest in pointing to areas of strength of civil society and hence of potential resistance to political authoritarianism. There are, of course, other examples, as a Chilean friend pointed out who had closely followed the (admittedly rather different) authoritarian politics of Thatcher in Britain and Pinochet in Chile and could point to the greater possibilities of resistance in the former case.

For the purposes of this book, what is interesting is the way in which conceptions of civil society have appealed to thinkers who would find a more traditional conception of society too solid, too Durkheimian, to be sustainable. Civil society theory foregrounds the associational dimension of society and politics, as in theories of associational democracy such as G.D.H. Cole's in the early twentieth century. It emphasizes the informal, the discursive aspects of social and political life rather than those formalized in social institutions and legally sanctioned constitutions. The connection to models of the public sphere is also particularly relevant to modern societies, in which political participation, for example, is increasingly mediated and virtual. For most of us, questioning political leaders is something we watch being done for us on television, rather than something we do ourselves in meeting halls.

The German philosopher and social theorist, Jürgen Habermas, who was a major impetus behind Cohen and Arato's analysis of civil society, is particularly interesting in this connection. Habermas began his career with an analysis of the rise and fall of the bourgeois public sphere. He traced the emergence of a critical public, well informed about public policy but without any formal part in its implementation, monitoring it from the salons and coffee-houses of eighteenth-century Europe, and the way in which this critical public opinion increasingly became, in the mid-twentieth century, an object of manipulation by political elites and what we have more recently come to call spin doctors. Over 30 years later, Habermas returned to the systematic analysis of processes of political communication which had preoccupied him in a more informal way throughout the intervening years, with a magisterial analysis of the relation between law and politics. Only political democracy can legitimate the law in a world where there are conflicting moral and legal principles, and

105

political democracy means not just formal representative institutions and practices but an ongoing dialogue between the more formal and the more informal parts of the political system. Whether a democracy functions properly depends not only on the formal relationships between institutions but on the quality of public debate:

> The social substratum for the realization of the system of rights consists neither in spontaneous market forces nor in the deliberate measures of the welfare state but in the currents of communication that, emerging from civil society and the public sphere, are converted into communicative power through democratic procedures. The fostering of autonomous public spheres, an expanded citizen participation, curbs on the power of the media, and the mediating function of political parties that are not simply elements of the state are of central signific- ance for this.[23]

For all this, however, it may be that the concept of civil society is too unstable in its location between public opinion or the public sphere, on the one hand, and more formal processes of political governance, on the other. Civil society in this associational sense, no less than in Hegel's very different sense of the term, tends to gravitate toward the state. The concept may, in other words be too vague to be helpful, except (and this is where the historical context of the 1980s shows its power as well as its limitations), where organized but informal groupings of people without formal power or institutional authority challenge established but somehow dis- credited institutions. It is no accident that two major current uses of the term are in the form of global civil society, anchored in an emergent world public opinion, world-wide human rights regimes and global social movements, including of course those opposed to (particular forms of) globalization, and in the invocation of a European civil society, following a similarly cosmopolitan agenda on a more limited though still quite substantial terrain. In both cases, the struc- tures of governance, the levels of state in Martin Shaw's terminology, are imprecise in their definition and in their interrelations. As a result, they are often more susceptible to effective informal influence or challenge before world public opinion than institutions more solidly entrenched within individual national states and correspondingly less open to dialogue with social movements whose *locus standi* is not clearly specified. The following chapter examines in more detail the European scene, where society and civil society have tended to be used interchangeably.

It remains the case, however, that those who baulk at using a full-blown concept of society may find the concept of civil society a useful, even inescapable resource, just as, more concretely, they may prefer to direct their political energies towards social movements rather than traditional political parties, whose continuing vitality, not least in the post-communist region, is something of a mystery to a 68er like me.[24]

8

Is There a European Society?

I have been defending a modest conception of society as sociation and suggesting that this can be identified both in very general terms, in which we speak of society in the singular, and in the differentiated form of what we still, *pace* the hyper-globalists, call societies. Among these a special place still belongs, despite everything, to the societies related to national (or sub-national) states. In Martin Shaw's words, quoted earlier, "it makes partial sense of talk of, say, British, Kurdish or Zulu society, as well as many other networks and sub-cultures of sub-national and transnational kinds."[1]

At the transnational end, a special place belongs also to the European integration process initiated very soon after World War II and resulting in the European Union of currently 25 member states.[2] The Union is of course large and growing: its population already exceeds that of the USA and Russia, the two superpowers of the second half of the twentieth century.[3] More importantly for this discussion, it raises questions about the nature of societies which in the nineteenth century were posed in a national framework (especially in Germany), but which now need to be rethought in more cosmopolitan terms. (It is this which justifies giving so much attention to Europe at the end of a book aimed only in part at European readers.) Thus, whereas the question at the head of this chapter would until the mid-twentieth century have tended to be given an answer in cultural, historical, or even, God help us, "racial" terms, it can now also be posed with reference to the political structure which includes now includes, directly or indirectly, most European states.[4]

We might now, in other words, apply the formula in Ernest Renan's classic essay, "What is a Nation?" to Europe in the sense of the EU. Renan's answer, phrased ostensibly at least in the terms of what we would now call civic as opposed to ethnic nationalism, was the following. After knocking down a succession of possible foundations of nationhood (geography, "race," language, religion, and so forth), Renan left his readers with two criteria to be jointly satisfied: the existence of a shared historical past and the ongoing will to remain part of a political community – what Renan calls, in rather flowery language, "a daily plebiscite."[5]

Thus, the United States, which is clearly one possible, if extreme, model for a federal European state, can and does invoke a shared past, going back for ideological purposes to the early European settlements, the Revolution or at least the Civil War, even if much of the population derives from more recent waves of immigration. And apart from a small number of Southern and other right-wing fanatics, there is no-one much calling for secession from the Union. Like Germany, the USA looks like a unified and, though large, relatively homogeneous nation-state, and we have at some time in our lives to be *told* that it actually has a federal structure in which the individual states have a certain amount of autonomy.

Renan's minimalist criteria have the advantage for Europeans that they do not have to give up on the idea of a European society or nation at the first hurdle because of linguistic, religious and ethnic diversity and messy boundaries. If anything, of course, the conventionally defined borders of Europe are, compared to those of most of its component states, as "natural" as they come. The famous British sea test applies for most of its circumference. You can sail, some of the year at least, from Archangel in the far North to Istanbul and anywhere you like on the Black Sea coast, taking in the "British" Isles and Iceland and leaving North Africa to starboard. The Urals, too, may not be much in the way of a barrier, but they can serve as a convenient marker. If you want to exclude

Russia because, for example, you are an anti-Russian Central or Eastern European, others may disagree but they will understand why; the same applies if you want to include the *whole* of Russia as far as the Pacific coast, as the EU will presumably do if and when it incorporates the Russian Federation as a member state or something close to one. And if, as I remember Derrida doing in conversation, you contemplate including New Zealand, again there is a kind of logic to the *démarche*.

Renan himself, of course, although he anticipated the replacement of the European nation-states by some sort of federation, would hardly have suggested that this could itself *become* a nation. It is useful, however, to push him a bit further against the grain and to pose his question in relation to European history and politics. Do Europeans have, or think they have, a common history? There is of course a good deal of interference on the European history channel, in the form of historical myths of Europe as some kind of demiurge like Botticelli's Venus, posing attractively against a fairly undifferentiated shell from which she rapidly extricates herself and goes on to greater things. A more adequate conception would of course be one in which the things which happen in the area which we have come to call Europe, a subcontinent of the Eurasian continent or subcontinent, occur in constant close interaction with more or less close neighbouring regions.[6]

But, one can respond with the kind of breathtaking cynicism which is best expressed in a single breath or sentence, perhaps what matters is not whether the myth of endogenous European development is false, but whether it is believed at some level by the European population. Taking this line, of course, we confront a further problem, that Europeans are also mostly trapped in "banal nationalist" histories in which European history is represented from a national perspective as essentially a history of national development and international conflict, internecine and often genocidal. And, of course, that's in part what it was. The question, then, becomes, once again, whether this sustains a sense of European identity, as opposed to, or as well as a national or sub-national one. Again, the cynical answer would be that history is written by the victors. *If* the European Union has emerged as a relatively harmonious federation, the history of what we call Europe will gradually fall into a Whiggish framework leading up to the post-war integration process. There are some signs of attempts to rewrite European history, especially for school students, along these lines and against the more familiar grain of separate national histories.

It is of course conflicts as much as anything else which have shaped the vague sense of Europeanness which, I suggest, can be seen as operating like a musical ground-bass in relation to the shrill rise and later decline of national identities in the nineteenth and twentieth centuries. In reflecting on the defining events and structures of European history, perhaps the most difficult issue is to decide at what point they are appropriately called European. Ancient Greek polyarchy as a form of intra- and interstate organization clearly deserves a mention, as do the Macedonian and, much more importantly, Roman empires. The latter of course intersects with a third crucial element, the somewhat improbable rise of Christianity in the Roman Empire and subsequently as a defining element of Europe as a whole, just as Islam became a defining element of the "Middle East."

Yet just as it is artificial to separate out English history from the rest of European history before the fifteenth century, it is similarly anachronistic to think of Europe as a distinct entity before that time. Charlemagne's empire of the early ninth century may have covered the territory of the original EC and lent his name to a building in Brussels and a prize awarded by the EU, but it had nothing to do with Europe as such. The Crusades of the thirteenth century are resented, with some justification, as inaugurating Europe's continuing domination of the "Middle East," but they are more appropriately seen, like the rest of the history of that half-millennium (and arguably the following one too), in a broader Eurasian context. A recent popular book features a map of the Hanseatic League labelled "The EU of the Middle Ages," but the irony is of course intentional.[7]

In what Europeans call the fifteenth and sixteenth centuries, however, something distinctively European begins to emerge, marked

111

by the conjuncture, roughly speaking, of the Renaissance, the Reformation and the beginnings of the voyages (anticipated of course by the Vikings) of discovery and conquest. These were not, to say the least, unique or endogenous "European" developments, but they do initiate a distinctive path: a line of development from the Renaissance to the scientific revolution and the Enlightenment, from the Reformation to the religious wars and the "European" state model consecrated in 1648 after perhaps the first genuinely European war, and from Columbian adventures to the European colonial and semi-colonial empires of the eighteenth, nineteenth and twentieth centuries. The "discoveries" were reflected in the culture shock of Europeans confronted by alterity and perceiving themselves in its mirror.[8] A different form of alterity closer to home was provided by the confrontation with the Turks at Mohács in 1526.

Whatever one might say about the more diffuse development of European conceptions of human and political rights and freedoms, the French Revolution clearly deserves a central place as the defining feature of the European political imaginary. This is no less true of the conservatives who rejected it or of the socialists and communists for whom it was just a prelude to a full social democratic and anti-capitalist revolution. Concurrently, the American Revolution inaugurated another form of republican constitutional government and, perhaps more importantly, the first major post-colonial state. For progressive Europeans, it was one more victory over the old aristocratic order, while geopolitically it marked the beginning of the provincialization of Europe, the relativization of its power in between the United States and Russia, which Tocqueville foresaw less than 40 years afterwards (and an even shorter time since Napoleon's short-lived European empire) and when Europe's imperial power was still on the rise. Imperialism, of course, transformed both Europe itself and much of the rest of the world, running alongside the generalization of capitalist production and industrialization. From now on, though few people were yet thinking in these terms (except perhaps in relation to the contrast between the Old and the New Worlds), there were multiple modernities and a post-European future.

Back at home, Europe changed in three major ways related to notions of citizenship. First, there was the slow extension of political democracy, finally reaching adult women in most parts of Europe in the early twentieth century. Second, nationalism arose in part as a reaction to Napoleon and consolidated the (Western) European nation-state model. This, with its prioritization of nation-state citizenship as a defining identity, swept the world wherever the European states had not established colonies or, as in South America, were expelled from them. Third, there was the dual response to the "social question" in the form of welfare states and social democracy. The former is the beginning of the "European social model" and social conceptions of citizenship, the latter of what can be called the European political model, the left–right division between ostensible opponents of, and all too real defenders of capitalism which structured European politics and tendentially the politics of much of the rest of the world at least until the end of the twentieth century. In Russia, of course, after the Bolshevik Revolution, there was only the left left. The thoroughly European ideology of Marxism took hold in Russia, China and elsewhere, with the Russian export model re-imported into much of Europe in the aftermath of World War II.

The world wars of the twentieth century were both quintessential expressions of Europe at its worst, practicing techniques of warfare often tried out earlier on colonized populations, and stages of its geopolitical decline. Earlier European wars had of course been fought outside Europe, but now wars could only be fought as world wars. The (nuclear) third world war which we escaped more by luck than anything else would of course have been a further and no doubt final example.

Geopolitically, the provincialization of Europe was marked by the subordination of most of the two halves of the divided continent into the Cold War military alliances firmly controlled from Washington and Moscow and by the withdrawal from almost all the colonized territories. Domestically, the three processes identified above modulated into the configuration in which we now live. Democracy was briskly extinguished in the communist bloc, only to bounce back 40 years later. In the West, there was a more diffuse democratization of social relations, particularly in the wake of the 1968 movements. Welfare states were further developed in both parts of Europe, though more slowly after the capitalist economic crisis of the mid-1970s. In the richer parts of the West, rights of abode and citizenship were more or less grudgingly accorded to the short- or long-term immigrants recruited to help out with the post-war boom of the *"trente glorieuses,"* the 30 glorious years. In another major social change, with the transformation of agriculture after World War II, the peasants who had been "nationalized" in Eugen Weber's sense in the late nineteenth century or collectivized in most of the Soviet bloc in the 1950s, were increasingly displaced into manufacturing or service occupations, leaving agricultural policy looking more like a disguised social policy to support the vestiges of rural life.[9]

Finally, and perhaps most dramatically, what began as a reaction to the consequences of nationalism in the two world wars developed gradually and haltingly into a new political model in Europe, an "ever closer union" of more and more European states whose ultimate destination or *finalité* remains more or less as unclear as when Andrew Shonfield examined it in 1973.[10] Briefly, however, and to anticipate what I shall say later, the EU is incipiently postnational, despite or because of its continuing symbiotic relationship with its member-states. It is post-imperial, in that however much it might superficially come to resemble something like the Austro-Hungarian Empire,[11] it will surely retain principles of democracy more characteristic of the national state. And it is perhaps (and this is part at least of its appeal), the beginning of a form of post-European cosmopolitan democracy attractive not just to Europe but to many other parts of the world.

What about Renan's second element: the continuing readiness to remain in a political community? Here, too, one could provisionally conclude that, with the exception of some parts of the populist right, notably the bizarre United Kingdom Independence Party and sections of the British Conservatives, the EU as a political formation is largely accepted. Unlike the nation-state, however, it is not the summit of the political landscape or even *primus inter pares*: it coexists with the polities of the member states, themselves federal to widely varying degrees. Only in the legal sphere is there something like a "normal" legal state with a hierarchy culminating in a federal Supreme Court, and that only for the limited, if growing, areas covered by EU law. And even here, the Court takes care not to present itself in such stark terms, for fear of upsetting public opinion in the member states.[12] At the other end of the legal spectrum, that of constitutional law, the EU confines itself to relatively vague acts of self-constitution.[13]

We are therefore confronted with a European polity which has a sort of Parliament, a sort of Supreme Court and a sort of Executive, but where none of the component parts is quite what or where it might be expected to be. As in the state socialist constitutions, there is a joker in the pack. There it was the ruling party; here it is the polymorphous Council of Ministers, emanating from the national governments of the member-states and functioning as a sort of non-parliamentary legislature. This situation is, of course, reflected in the political profile of the EU, the famous "democratic deficit." Say "Parliament," and Europeans think, depending on their national location, of Westminster, of the Chambre des Députés, of the Cortes, of the Bundestag or of the Sejm, rather than of the European Parliament in Brussels/Luxemburg/Strasbourg.[14]

Many of the most creative and perceptive analysts of the European scene have drawn the conclusion that we should stop thinking in terms of state (or polity), society (or civil society), and so on, and think in less ambitious categories such as transnational social practices. Michael Mann poses the issue with characteristic clarity: "Is there a Society Called Euro?." As he stresses, summarizing his longstanding work on the history of power which parallels that by Anthony Giddens referred to earlier:

There has never been a singular systemic network of social interaction which might constitute, as it were, "a total society" . . . Human societies have always consisted of multiple, overlapping intersecting networks of interaction each with differing boundaries and rhythms of development . . . Just as there never was a nation-state society, just as . . . there is not a global society, nor can there be a singular society called Euro, only at maximum a European network of interaction at the boundaries of which occurs a limited degree of cleavage.[15]

Even in this modest sense, Mann suggests, European networks of ideological, economic and military power, though growing, are relatively weak, especially if they are compared to the broader scale of "the North as a whole."[16]

Chris Rumford draws a similarly sceptical conclusion:

Within the discourses of European civil society . . . the idea of a unitary societal order still dominates.

. . . the preference for talking of a European *civil* society seems doubly naïve, given its association not simply with the society of the nation-state, but more importantly with an integrated and structured community of interest.[17]

From this perspective, the concepts of society and civil society are inextricably bound up with the frame of reference of the nation-state, and any attempt to project them onto a European frame will merely reproduce this on a larger scale in a way which is both sociologically and politically naïve. Sociologically or generally, because so-called societies are no longer unified in this way. Politically or specifically, because there is no conceivable prospect of Europe in particular achieving this kind or degree of integration. The first objection points to the entrenched methodological nationalism of social science: the spurious identification of society with an ideally integrated model of the nation-state (and, perhaps, its culture). The second emphasizes its real-world counterpart: what Michael Billig has aptly characterized as "banal nationalism."[18]

Billig points out the extent to which nation-state categories frame our social experience and our most basic assumptions. Flags, public holidays, weather forecasts, and so on are all cast in these categories.[19]

116

This is not national*ism* in a strong sense, but rather the unthinking adoption of the nation-state frame of reference. This has clear and disappointing implications for Europe or the EU as an imagined community. The symbols, the reference points, will almost always tend to be national rather than European. The Euro is of course an important counter-example, though even here the national inflection of the coinage and the deliberate vagueness of the architectural images on the banknotes combine to weaken the European message. It is also clear, as a lot of the literature on globalization has noted, that international or supranational processes are characteristically *experienced* at a local (which often means a national) level. In Europe, for example, customs tariffs may be a matter of European-level policy, but they are largely imposed by locally employed staff of member states, for reasons of convenience and tradition.[20] The upshot of Billig's book for reflection on European integration is to suggest that the road slopes more steeply uphill than we may sometimes have thought.

And yet, we may say in a slightly pale Galilean way, something of a societal kind *is* moving at the level of the EU, the European Economic Area or Europe as a whole. There is a clear prospect, and in many member-states already the reality, of a common currency and a shared area of border-free travel. There is a shared legal framework in the form of European human rights and EU law, equal rights for non-nationals or non-residents to medical treatment and some social security benefits, and so on. Levels of migration, travel, intermarriage, and so on between member-states are of course very low by North American standards but by no means negligible. A European or global frame of reference in the presentation of statistical indicators and other data has become much more common than in the past.

Cultural consumption, too, has become more cosmopolitan, with television viewers increasingly accessing internationally oriented channels such as CNN, BBC World or Al-Jazeera rather than local ones. Although there is no genuinely European newspaper, published in the major languages, and *The European* (1990–98), published in

English and owned for most of its brief life by the notorious entre-
preneur Robert Maxwell, made a poor showing compared to the
Herald Tribune, The Financial Times or *The Economist,* the substantial
pan-European presence of these three publications is perhaps the
beginning of a more integrated media scene. There is also a good
deal of syndication along the US pattern, and more systematic relations between *The Guardian, Le Monde, The Washington Post* and
other papers.[21]

One can also identify a process of convergence, often called
"Europeanization" between institutions and elites in government,
business, and a whole range of other social spheres. The British
historian, Keith Middlemas offered an early analysis, before the term
Europeanization was entrenched in the discourse, of this kind of
informal cooperation (in the non-technical sense) within the EC/EU:

> The game also induces a process of socialization, habituating players to
> each other, forcing them to think through other points of view and
> subsequently live with them. Indeed, this Euro-civilising aspect may
> come to be seen . . . as informal politics' largest contribution to the
> European Union.[22]

A discussion of European society or civil society necessarily hangs
between the two poles of questions about broadly conceived European cultural identities, on the one hand, and European-level economic and political institutions and practices, of the kind described
above, on the other. My approach to these questions is therefore
something like that advanced by Habermas in 1974 in an early
reflection on the possibilities of social identities not tied to territorial
states and their membership. A collective identity, Habermas argues,
can only be conceived in a reflexive form, in an awareness that one
has opportunities to participate in

> processes of communication in which identity formation occurs as
> a continuous learning process. Such value and norm creating
> communications . . . flow out of the "base" into the pores of

118

organizationally structured areas of life. They have a subpolitical character, i.e. they operate below the level of political decision processes, but they indirectly influence the political system because they change the normative framework of political decisions.[23]

Although Habermas does not make the connection here, there are clear parallels between this approach emerging out of his theory if communicative action, and analyses by Karl Deutsch (1912–92) and others of integration processes emerging out of, and substantially constituted by, communication. "By integration we mean the attainment, within a territory, of a 'sense of community' and of institutions and practices strong enough and widespread enough to assure, for a 'long' time, dependable expectations of 'peaceful change'."[24]

These "practices" take two overlapping forms in particular: transactions and communications. There is probably not much point in formally specifying the differences between these.[25] The frequency of Europe-level actions and interactions, as opposed to "domestic" ones, can act as a marker of the degree to which transactions and communications take place across national borders. As Jan Delhey points out, the ideal reference point is clear enough:

> European social integration would be fully achieved if intergroup relations between the EU nationalities were mutually as frequent and cohesive as in-group relations within these nationalities – in this case, the component parts of the European social space would be dissolved because Europeans act (and think) like citizens of one single nation. Obviously, Europe is far away from such a degree of integration.[26]

Here, then, is a promising set of proposals for investigating Europeanness from the bottom, in empirical terms. There is, I think, at least enough going on to be measurable, and to encourage attempts such as that in the present chapter to construct a meaningful concept of European society or civil society. To get closer to this, we have, I think, to see it as stretched between the historical and present-day cultural commonalities of what we now call Europe and the emergent, fragmentary and contested European state or polity. As Ulrich Beck and Edgar Grande argue at length, a reflective and cosmopolitan conception of Europe can to some extent escape the dilemmas of in/out, us/them, nation-state/federation.[27]

I share Habermas' view that modernity should be seen, among other things, as an unfinished and, indeed, open-ended project. Most importantly, the element of self-reflection which I would argue is built into the discourse of modernity implies that all our practices and ways of life are in principle open to questioning and attempts to justify them. They become, in Habermas' sense, post-conventional. Habermas has, for example, defended a conception of "constitutional patriotism" based not on membership of a particular ethnic or national community or *Volk* but on a rational and defensible identification with a decent constitutional state which may of course happen to be the one whose citizenship one holds.

I am assuming, on the basis of the argument of the previous chapters, that we can meaningfully talk about the existence of socie*ties* and civil socie*ties*, however embattled, in most if not all of Europe. Whether there is also an emergent *European* society or civil society is a further question. Without overplaying conceptions of identity and pursuing the chimera of a European *Staatsvolk*, a "people" which would underpin the European "state," I think that to talk of a European civil society does presuppose some minimal version of a European identity, perhaps a weak or "thin" cultural identity based on a particular modulation of modernity.

There are, as I suggested in the previous chapter, good reasons to focus not just on the associational dimension of society or civil society but on its interaction with other political and economic (and even military) structures in relation to the integration process. This is not to justify the dangerous elitism of much European integration politics, with its shameless technocratism, its somewhat sinister reference to the *acquis communautaire* and its neglect or patronizing of the benighted natives, but it does suggest an open-minded and broad-spectrum approach to Europe-level activities. A European identity may emerge from conflicts in agricultural negotiations and the battles against BSE ("mad cow disease") and "foot and mouth" as well as from more lofty exercises in pursuit of common values.

I believe that one can ask meaningful questions about the degree to which cultures, understood in the broadest sense as including material elements such as systems of production as well as those more often assigned to the domain of "culture," are unified or diversified. If I board a train at Waterloo Station in London, things are very different at my destination depending whether I travel to Southampton or to Lille, even if the journey time is about the same. Both cities, however, also have features in common which would distinguish them from comparable cities in, say, India.

What can be said in the end about the residual distinctiveness of Europe as a cultural region of the modern world? A familiar theme, invoked even in an advertising series by Shell a few years ago, is diversity, notably the diversity of languages. Compared to the largely Anglophone societies of North America or the area sharing Chinese pictograms, or even large regions such as India or the former USSR with an established lingua franca, Europe looks rather a mess. One may wonder how far such a perception rests on overlooking linguistic diversity elsewhere in the world, but Michael Mann may well be right that what counts is the combination of competition between smallish units under the unifying umbrella of Christendom.[28] It is at least true that in the European case a pattern of linguistic variation largely coexisting with the boundaries of developed modern states creates powerful entrenched structures and interests which in turn, act as obstacles to cultural and political integration.[29]

Europe's position as a major cultural producer is of course one of the effects of its previous world hegemony, partly preserved in that of its world languages: English, French, Spanish, Portuguese and, to some extent, even Dutch. It has also stood up in many ways to the challenge of North American imports. This applies not just to cultural commodities such as films but also to material aspects of life such as the car-based civilization; despite everything, most European cities remain less car-based and suburbanized than US ones. For a time these might have seemed like cultural lags. Now, however, it appears

121

that in many ways parts of the USA are returning to more "European" modes of life, including railways and urban mass transit systems, delicatessen food (even cheese) and niche markets for cult movies in some of the cities. And if there is, as Colin Crouch once suggested,[30] a European model or set of models of industrial relations, this may well appeal to other regions of the world. (In the European context, the UK governments of Thatcher and Major were out on a limb in wanting to abandon some of the benefits of the European system and adopt largely misunderstood Asian models instead.) Europe also appears "modern" in relation to the USA and many other regions of the world in the extent of its secularization: whatever the difficulties of measurement in this domain, it is clear that religious belief in Europe has mostly ceased to have the kind of importance for social life as a whole which it has retained elsewhere, even in ostensibly secular states such as the USA or India.

A European identity will also be something highly mediated in the sense of virtual, where the real agents are likely to remain predominantly drawn from a limited number of social circles; as Richard Münch puts it, somewhat brutally, "the elites of top managers, experts, political leaders and intellectuals)."[31] This applies, *par excellence*, of course, to the EU's own elites: as Beck and Grande note, the EU embodies the paradox of a civil society *from above* aiming to establish one from below.[32] More optimistically, they suggest, the concept of European civil society offers the EU the opportunity of opening up a transnational space in such a way that it organizes itself.

We may wish, then, for a "people's Europe" beyond the glass and print temples of the EU institutions, but this will have to develop in some sort of relation with them, rather as communists used to have to define themselves, whether positively or negatively, in relation to the Soviet Union. For most Europeans inside the EU, and to some extent outside it as well, it is now the dominant European political form and representation, even if they rightly feel that there is more to Europe, both intensionally and extensionally, than the EU.

With the collapse of the "people's democracies," and the eclipse of revolutionary socialism, the liberal democratic state, like capitalism, has no obvious practical alternative. If anything, and despite very important elements of disillusionment or political alienation, it has acquired stronger roots with the democratization of everyday life: the growing acceptance, exemplified in spheres as diverse as media interviews with politicians and child-rearing practices, that all our decisions and ways of life are in principle open to questioning. They become, in Habermas' sense, "post-conventional." Individualism of this kind may also, as Richard Münch has suggested,[33] favor the development of a European identity. The more sovereign and reflexive we are in the construction of our individual identities, the easier it may be for us to incorporate, or even to foreground, a European one.

Banal supranationalism, transnationalism or postnationalism are, however, arguably what we need: the increasing adoption, though not necessarily unreflectively, of a Europe-wide frame of reference for the discussion of political and other social issues. Like Tocqueville, we can go to America to see what this might look like in a European context. Or we can look at countries like Italy where, for historical and ongoing reasons to do with the nature of the Italian state, regional and European identities and reference-points are stronger than in many other member-states of the Union. And one can look at social movements and their cosmopolitan forms of knowledge and practice.

Once again, Europe is pioneering a mode of governance, this time transnational rather than national, which gives some practical embodiment to the current extension of democratic thinking into conceptions of cosmopolitan democracy. This development, which Habermas has called "Europe's second chance,"[34] is as important, I believe, as the earlier extension of liberal democracy into social democracy; it coexists uneasily, however, with communitarian thinking both in social and political philosophy and in the practice of, for example, Clinton and Blair, and to some extent Jospin and Schröder. In the political sphere, Habermas in *The Postnational Constitution*, has, as noted above, popularized Dolf Sternberger's conception of "constitutional patriotism" (*Verfassungspatriotismus*) based on a rational identification with a constitutional state. But as Habermas has also come to stress, if the liberal democratic nation-state has few internal enemies, it is increasingly seen as inappropriate to the contemporary reality of global processes and challenges as well as to the desire of many citizens for more local autonomy.

In this postnational constellation, as Habermas has called it, the progress of European union, combined as it is with attempts to strengthen regional autonomy under the slogan of "subsidiarity," becomes a crucial external determinant of the internal reconfiguration of many European states, notably the UK. We may gradually be coming to think of European society in the same flexible and non-exclusive way as we may now speak of Scottish or British society.

Postscript
A Defensible Concept of "Society"

God is dead.
No; he's alive and well and working on a less ambitious project.
(Anonymous graffiti exchange)

Something like this, I suggest, might be said of our conception of society in the early twenty-first century. The old idea of the social body and the vocabulary of health and sickness are slipping out of use, as is the unthinking identification of "society" with the national state. Our sense of concern for others, uneven and unstable as it may be, is increasingly global and, in Europe, sometimes European. Despite the appeal of political and economic reductionism, especially in the neo-liberal decades of the 1980s and 1990s, there remains a sense of the importance of the social dimension. As recent developments in post-communist Europe and elsewhere have reminded us, polities and markets do not operate in a vacuum; the density and quality of social relations – civil society in a broad sense of the term – form a crucial background. Cultural processes, too, are not entirely free-floating, even if they are "weightless."

Whether or not we are anarchists, we understand what is meant by the idea of "Society against the state" in the sense of Tom Paine, Pierre Clastres, or Alain Touraine, and we see it on the streets, recently in Ukraine and Kyrgyzstan, where sustained popular protest overturned the result of rigged elections, and tomorrow somewhere else.

125

A longstanding tradition of thought, particularly strong perhaps in Europe and the other regions of the world most influenced by it, opposes individualism and cosmopolitanism to "society"; another seems them as mutually compatible in a borderless or only contingently bordered republic or some other form of community. What Beck has called the cosmopolitan view or vision makes possible a reconceptualization of social and political theory on a genuinely universalistic basis, as opposed to the false universalism which projected the national state or society onto the world or abstractly rejected the former in favor of the latter. Perhaps we can move beyond the either/or dichotomies of state/society, individual/society and so on to more flexible conceptualizations of both. This would be a genuinely social imaginary for the still new century and millennium, and one which can justifiably engage our imagination.

Notes

Preface

1   For an interesting recent exercise in this genre, whose subtitle I unwittingly borrowed, see Phillip Brown and Hugh Lauder, *Capitalism and Social Progress: The Future of Society in a Global Economy* (Basingstoke: Palgrave, 2001).
2   See Chapter 2 in this volume.
3   See Chapter 3 in this volume.
4   See Chapter 4 in this volume.
5   See Chapter 5 in this volume.
6   Zygmunt Bauman, *Society under Siege* (Cambridge: Polity, 2002). The cover, rather mysteriously, shows the waterfront of Cologne overshadowed from behind by an enormous wave.
7   See, for example, Craig Calhoun, "Indirect Relationships and Imagined Communities: Large-Scale Social Integration and the Transformation of Everyday Life", in Pierre Bourdieu and James S. Coleman (eds.), *Social Theory for a Changing Society* (Boulder, CO: Westview Press, 1991). The term "imagined communities" is of course drawn from Benedict Anderson's classic work, *Imagined Communities: Reflections on the Origin and Spread of Nationalism* (London: New Left Books, 1983). For a recent account of representations of the state, see Mark Neocleous, *Imagining the State* (Maidenhead: Open University Press, 2003).

Chapter 1 The Origins of "Society"

1   The Durkheimian sociologist Marcel Granet's *La pensée chinoise* (Paris: La Renaissance du Livre, 1934) remains a fundamental reference. See also Wang Hui, "Imagining Asia. A Genealogical Analysis," forthcoming in 2005; previewed in *Le monde diplomatique* (Feb. 2005), pp. 20–2.

127

2   See Chapter 7 in this volume.
3   See, for example, William Outhwaite, "Social Thought and Social Science," *New Cambridge Modern History*, vol. XIII (Companion Volume) (Cambridge: Cambridge University Press 1979), pp. 271–92. The term "long Enlightenment" reflects the current tendency of Enlightenment historians to stretch it both backwards and forwards from the "core" decades of the eighteenth century.
4   Keith Michael Baker, "Enlightenment and the Institution of Society," in Sudipta Kaviraj and Sunil Khilnani (eds.), *Civil Society. History and Possibilities* (Cambridge: Cambridge University Press, 2001). See also Baker, "Enlightenment and the Institution of Society: Notes for a Conceptual History," in W. Melching and W. Velema (eds.), *Main Trends in Cultural History* (Amsterdam: Rodopi, 1994).
5   David Frisby and Derek Sayer, *Society* (Chichester: Ellis Horwood, 1986).
6   J.-J. Rousseau, "A Discourse on the Origin of Inequality among Men," Preface, in Rousseau, *The Social Contract and the Discourses*, trans. G.D.H. Cole (London: Dent, [1754] 1913), p. 155.
7   Frisby and Sayer, *Society*, p. 22. Cf. Baron de Montesquieu, *L'esprit des lois*, Book 1, Chapter 1 (Paris: Edition-Touquet, 1821), p. 6.
8   And even here, it can be argued, to establish the concept of society was an uphill struggle. See the article by Daniela Barberis, "In Search of an Object: Organicist Sociology and the Reality of Society in *Fin-de-siècle* France," *History of the Human Sciences* 16: 3 (2003), pp. 51–72.
9   Quoted by Theodor Adorno in Frankfurt Institute for Social Research, *Aspects of Sociology* (London: Heinemann, 1973), p. 17.
10 For a fuller discussion, see Chapter 5 in this volume, pp. 72–3.
11 See, for example, Peter C. Ludz, "Die Bedeutung der Soziologie für die politische Wissenschaft: Zur wissenschaftssoziologischen Interpretation des Streites um die politische Soziologie in den fünfziger Jahren," in G. Lüschen (ed.), *Deutsche Soziologie seit 1945, Kölner Zeitschrift für Soziologie und Sozialpsychologie*, Sonderheft 21 (Opladen: Westdeutscher Verlag, 1979), pp. 264–93.
12 Marx, *Grundrisse. Foundations of the Critique of Political Economy (Rough Draft)* (Harmondsworth: Penguin, 1973), p. 94.
13 Ibid., pp. 100–1. The Austro-Marxist Max Adler suggested that "the central concept of Marxist sociology is not society but socialised humanity." "The Relation of Marxism to Classical German Philosophy," in Tom Bottomore and Patrick Goode (eds.), *Austro-Marxism* (Oxford: Clarendon Press, 1978), p. 65. See Chapter 6 in this volume.
14 Ibid., p. 106.
15 Michel Foucault, in a series of lectures in 1976, argued that these concepts of society and nation emerge out of the reaction of the nobility to the absolutist

monarchy, taking the form of a counter-history of France. In contrast to the traditional conception of the nation as the totality of the Monarch's subjects:

> according to history as written by [Henry de] Boulainvilliers, all that was required for the nation to exist were men who were brought together by certain interests, and who had a certain number of things in common, such as customs, habits, and possibly a language. (Foucault, *Society Must Be Defended*, London: Allen Lane, 2003, p. 218)

This broad concept of the nation is then taken up by the bourgeoisie and, in a different form, by Marxist and fascist critics of bourgeois society. "It is this notion of a nation that gives rise to notions like nationality, race, and class" (ibid., p. 142).

16 See p. 132; n. 4.

17 *The Principles of Sociology*, vol. I, part II, chapter II (London: Williams and Norgate, 1893), p. 437.

18 Ibid., pp. 557ff. He qualified these claims, however, by insisting that:

> there exist no analogies between the body politic and a living body, save those necessitated by the mutual dependence of parts which they display in common. Though, in foregoing chapters, sundry comparisons of social structures and functions in the human body have been made, they have been made only because structures and functions in the human body furnish familiar illustrations of structures and functions in general. The social organism, discrete instead of concrete, asymmetrical instead of symmetrical, sensitive in all its units instead of having a single sensitive centre, is not comparable to any particular type of social organism, animal or vegetal. (ibid., p. 580)

A useful discussion of these issues can be found in Karl Mannheim's essay, "The Concept of the State as an Organism," in his *Essays on Sociology and Social Psychology* (London: Routledge, 1953).

19 *The Rules of Sociological Method* (London: Macmillan, 1982). First published in 1895.

20 *Suicide: A Sociological Study* (London: Routledge, 1963). First published in 1897.

21 *The Division of Labor in Society* (London: Macmillan, 1984). First published in 1893.

22 Daniela Barberis, "In Search of an Object," explores the importance of these images for "establishing a strong notion of society as a concrete, real entity" (p. 51).

23 On this concept, see the definitive collection of essays edited by W.S.F. Pickering, *Durkheim and Representations* (London: Routledge, 2000). As Frisby and Sayer note (*Society*, pp. 75−9), this conception brings Durkheim closer to positions such as Georg Simmel's discussed below.

24 The French term is of course ambiguous between these two senses.
25 As Durkheim put it in a review of a book by the Italian Marxist Antonio Labriola (*Revue Philosophique* 44, 1897, pp. 645–51),

> We believe it a fruitful idea that social life must be explained not by the conception of it formed by those who participate in it, but by profound causes which escape their consciousness. We also think that these causes must be sought mainly in the way in which the associated individuals are grouped.

See also "Note: Morphologie sociale," *L'Année Sociologique* 2, 1899, pp. 520–1.
26 *Suicide*, trans. p. 212.
27 *Rules*, trans., p. xli (translation modified).
28 Stedman Jones, "Representation in Durkheim's Masters: Kant and Renouvier," in Pickering, *Durkheim and Representations*, p. 71.
29 *L'Education morale* (Paris: Alcan, 1925), p. 318.
30 Tönnies, *Der Nietzsche-Kultus: eine Kritik* (Leipzig: O.R. Reisland, 1897).
31 See my essay, "Nietzsche and Critical Theory," in Peter Sedgwick (ed.), *Nietzsche: A Critical Reader* (Oxford: Blackwell, 1995); and Franz Solms-Laubach, *Nietzsche and Early German and Austrian Sociology* (Berlin and New York, De Gruyter).
32 Kurt Wolff (ed.), *Georg Simmel* (Columbus, OH: Ohio State University Press, 1959), p. 338.
33 The title of a substantial essay, "The Concept and Tragedy of Culture," in G. Simmel, *The Conflict in Modern Culture and Other Essays* (original edn. 1911; New York: Teachers College Press, 1968), pp. 27–46.
34 Cited in, for example, Wolfgang Mommsen, *The Age of Bureaucracy* (Oxford: Blackwell, 1974), p. 110.
35 One place where Weber may be taken to be implicitly criticizing Durkheim is at the beginning of his collected essays on the sociology of religion, where he says that a definition of religion (such as Durkheim had offered) cannot possibly come at the beginning but only at the end of the investigation. Here Weber sides implicitly with Nietzsche's view that only things which have no history can be defined.
36 Weber, *Roscher and Knies* (New York: Free Press, 1975).
37 Translations include *The Problems of the Philosophy of History* (1892) (New York: Free Press, 1977). See David Frisby, *Georg Simmel*. London: Routledge, Revised Edition 2002.
38 Georg Simmel, *Über soziale Differenzierung* (Leipzig: Duncker & Humblot, 1890), p. 10; cf. Frisby and Sayer, *Society*, p. 56.
39 *Economy and Society* (New York: Bedminster Press, 1968), vol. I, p. 18.
40 See Arthur Mitzman, *Sociology and Estrangement: Three Sociologists of Imperial Germany* (New York: Knopf, 1973).

41 Marx and Engels, *Manifesto of the Communist Party* (1848) (London: Penguin 1967), p. 79.

42 Letter to Weydemeyer, March 5, 1852, in *Marx-Engels Collected Works* (London: Lawrence and Wishart, 1975), vol. 39, p. 58.

43 Marx, *Capital*, vol. III (Harmondsworth: Penguin, 1976), p. 927.

44 Jacques Donzelot, *L'Invention du social* (Paris: Fayard, 1984).

45 According to H. Silver and F. Wilkinson:

> In line with the Republican ideology of solidarity, problems like long-term unemployment and rising poverty were construed as manifestations of "social exclusion" or "a rupture of the social bond". Thus, even the names of new French policies reflected the goals of "insertion", "integration", "cohesion" and "solidarity" . . . Except in academic circles, British social policy discourse used the terminology of long-term "dependency", "new poverty", and the "underclass", problems to be combated with "self-reliance", "enterprise", "opportunity", "citizenship", "partnerships" and "community".

("Policies to Combat Social Exclusion: A French-British Comparison", in G. Rogers et al., *Social Exclusion*, Geneva: International Institute for Labour Studies, 1995, p. 285)

46 Werner Sombart, *Why is There No Socialism in the United States?* (London: Macmillan, 1976).

47 *Political Parties: A Sociological Study of the Oligarchical Tendencies of Modern Democracy* (New York: Free Press, 1962).

48 See Mitzman, *Sociology and Estrangement.*

49 The term "radical democracy," introduced by Ernesto Laclau and Chantal Mouffe and adopted also by Jürgen Habermas, reflects a sense that capitalism is "the only game in town"; this capitulation or accommodation is counterbalanced for Habermas and others by a more ambitious notion of cosmopolitan democracy, discussed in Chapter 4.

50 See the classic study by Jean Pierre Faye, *Les Langages totalitaires* (Paris: Hermann, 1972).

51 Engels, *Anti-Dühring*, Marx-Engels-Werke (Berlin: Dietz, 1962), vol. 20, p. 262.

52 *Division of Labor in Society.*

53 Radcliffe-Brown, *Structure and Function in Primitive Society: Essays and Addresses* (London: Cohen and West, 1952), p. 43.

54 Kingsley Davis, "The Myth of Functional Analysis as a Special Method in Sociology and Anthropology," *American Sociological Review* 24: 6 (December 1959), pp. 757–72. Cf. W.E. Moore, "Functionalism," in Tom Bottomore and Robert Nisbet (eds.), *A History of Sociological Analysis* (New York: Basic Books, 1978). For an excellent overview of functionalism, see John Holmwood,

"Functionalism and its Critics," in Austin Harrington (ed.), *Modern Social Theory: An Introduction* (Oxford University Press, 2005), pp. 87–109.

55 Even the sociobiology of the 1970s and 1980s was individualistic in its emphasis.

56 See David Lockwood, "Social Integration and System Integration," in G.K. Zollschan and W. Hirsch (eds.), *Explorations in Social Change* (London: Routledge, 1964). pp. 244–57.

57 What was known as "Conflict Theory," drawing on Marx and Weber and associated particularly with the work of John Rex and Ralf Dahrendorf, was constituted as the opposite pole to functionalism; Lockwood's discussion is still worth reading on this. The German-American (and Simmelian) sociologist Lewis Coser offered an important functionalist response in *The Functions of Social Conflict* (New York: Free Press, 1956).

58 For critiques of the anti-political implications of system theory, see Sheldon Wolin, *Politics and Vision* (Boston: Little, Brown, 1960), Pierre Birnbaum, *La fin du politique* (Paris: Seuil, 1975) and Jürgen Habermas and Niklas Luhmann, *Theorie der Gesellschaft oder Sozialtechnologie?* (Frankfurt: Suhrkamp, 1971).

59 As Bruno Latour put it in a recent interview, "Nature" and "Society" are "cheap" ways of analyzing the connections between things which overlook their singularity ("The Social as Association," in Nicholas Gane (ed.), *The Future of Social Theory*, London and New York: Continuum, 2004, p. 87). See also Chapter 6, in this volume.

Chapter 2 Society and the Individual

1 *Women's Own* magazine, October 3, 1987. The context was, however, one in which she was arguing that people should be self-reliant and not expect help from "society."

2 *Our Island Story: A History of England for Boys and Girls*, by H.E. Marshall; with pictures by A.S. Forrest (London: T.C. & E.C. Jack, 1905).

3 Robert Nisbet, *The Sociological Tradition* (New York: Basic Books, 1966).

4 In the UK, for example, Margaret Thatcher and Keith Joseph came close to abolishing the Social Science Research Council on the grounds that there was no such thing as social science; the SSRC was reprieved but under the more anodyne label of the Economic and Social Research Council (which of course also indicated their favoritism towards economics).

5 See, for example, G. Becker, *The Economics of Life* (New York: McGraw-Hill, 1996).

6 David Hume, *An Enquiry Concerning Human Understanding* (1748), section VIII. ed. T.H. Green (London: 1889), p. 68.

7   Mancur Olsen, *The Logic of Collective Action* (Cambridge, MA: Harvard University Press, 1965).

8   James Coleman, *Foundations of Social Theory* (Cambridge, MA: Harvard University Press, 1990).

9   Martin Hollis, *Models of Man* (Cambridge: Cambridge University Press, 1977), p. 21.

10 Martin Hollis and Steve Smith, *Explaining and Understanding International Relations* (Oxford: Oxford University Press, 1990).

11 Becker, *The Economic Approach to Human Behavior* (Chicago: University of Chicago Press, 1976), p. 7.

12 G. Therborn, *Between Sex and Power: Family in the World 1900–2000* (London: Routledge, 2004), p. 5.

13 Lukes here (1970, p. 77) and in his book *Individualism* (Oxford: Blackwell, 1973, Chapter 17) deals rather too briskly, as I suggest below, with methodological individualism.

14 José López and John Scott, in *Social Structure* (Buckingham: Open University Press, 2000), provide an excellent overview of some of these differences in relation to social structure, while arguing, I think rightly, for a synthetic conception which links them together in alliance with, rather than opposition to, the concept of action (see ibid., pp. 106–7).

15 Hans Vaihinger, *The Philosophy of As-If*, trans. C.K. Ogden (London: Kegan Paul, 1924).

16 Pierre Bourdieu, *Outline of a Theory of Practice* (Cambridge: Cambridge University Press, 1974).

17 According to Touraine, in *Sociologie de l'action*: "In societies with weak historicity, the human being can only put some order into an experience which his or her reason does not master" (Paris: Seuil, 1965), p. 69. "When, however, economic development appears as a desire for change and for the overcoming of social and cultural obstacles expected gradually to decompose, it is natural for social thought to approach the sociology of action" (ibid., p. 96). My translations.

18 Hayek, *The Counter-Revolution in Science: Studies on the Abuse of Reason* (New York: Free Press, 1955), p. 56.

19 Popper, *The Poverty of Historicism* (London: Routledge and Kegan Paul, 1957), p. 140.

20 Rom Harré, *Social Being* (Oxford: Blackwell, 1979), p. 237. He glosses this on p. 349 as follows: "After all I am trying to locate the social psychological processes and not to solve the great traditional problems of sociology!" [Harré's exclamation mark] Some 15 years after *Social Being*, in *Varieties of Realism*, Harré presents a similar argument in broader terms. Social structures are not actually or even potentially observable: they are part of a class of "beings

which, if real, could not become phenomena for human observers, however well equipped with devices to amplify and extend the senses" (Oxford: Blackwell, 1986), p. 73.

21 According to Harré:

> Believing in the transpersonal reality of social structure and taking for granted that social structures could be causally efficacious, reformist minded Critical Realists [among whom he includes Roy Bhaskar, Alan Norrie, Margaret Archer and myself] have slipped back into the frame of mind that very quickly degenerates into bureaucratic socialism. ("Causal Mechanism and Social Practices," unpublished conference paper presented at Brunel University, November 1999, p. 1)

22 He tends, however, to add that he does not actually believe in social structures.
23 Harré, "Causal Mechanism and Social Practices," p. 2; cf. Harré, "Social Reality and the Myth of Social Structure," *European Journal of Social Theory*, 5, 1, Feb. 2002, p. 112.
24 "Causal Mechanism," p. 14.
25 "Social Reality and the Myth of Social Structure," p. 112.
26 Ibid., p. 117.
27 Ibid., p. 114, original emphasis.
28 See the comments following Harré's article by Piet Strydom and Bob Carter. Piet Strydom, "Is the Social Scientific Concept of Structure a Myth? A Critical Response to Harré" *European Journal of Social Theory* 5 (2002), pp. 124–33; Bob Carter, "People Power: Harré and the Myth of Social Structure," *European Journal of Social Theory* 5 (2002), pp. 134–42.
29 *Social Being*, p. 94.
30 David Lockwood, "Social Integration and System Integration" (1964).
31 Weber, *Economy and Society*, vol. 1 (New York: Bedminster Press, 1968), p. 7, translated as in W.G. Runciman (ed.), *Max Weber: Selections in Translation* (Cambridge: Cambridge University Press, 1978), pp. 17–18.
32 See, for example, Emile Durkheim, *The Elementary Forms of the Religious Life* (original edn. 1912; New York: Free Press, 1995); Paul Veyne, *Did the Greeks Believe in Their Myths?* (Chicago: University of Chicago Press, 1988).
33 See José López and Gary Potter (eds.), *After Postmodernism: An Introduction to Critical Realism* (London: Athlone, 2001), Chapter 1, for an interesting exchange between Harré and Bhaskar and other realists.
34 Peter Berger and Thomas Luckmann, *The Social Construction of Reality. An Essay in the Sociology of Knowledge* (Harmondsworth: Penguin, 1966), p. 15.
35 Berger and Luckmann's relativistic sociology of knowledge has been somewhat overshadowed by the rise of postmodernism in the 1980s. Lyotard's influential book, *The Postmodern Condition: A Report on Knowledge* was published in 1979 and in English in 1984, but it was his more skeptical work on

language games, along with Derrida's program of "deconstruction" and what came to be known in the English-speaking world as post-structuralism, which gave a new impetus to social constructionism. Many of the themes of what is now presented as postmodern sociology were, however, already present in ethnomethodology and the sociology of knowledge, as well as in other developments out of hermeneutics and the philosophy of language.

36 *The Social Construction of Reality*, p. 96. Berger and Luckmann offer a strikingly different account of the notion of reification from that in Lukács' Marxist analysis. Whereas, for Lukács, it denotes a material process grounded in cap-italism and commodity fetishism, here it means essentially our "forgetting" that reality is socially constructed. This sedimented knowledge becomes some-thing like a material reality. According to Berger and Luckmann: "If the integration of an institutional order can be understood only in terms of the 'knowledge' that its members have of it, it follows that the analysis of such 'knowledge' will be essential for an analysis of the institutional order in question" (pp. 82–3).

37 "How is it possible that human activity (*Handeln*) should produce a world of things (*choses*)?" (ibid., p. 30).

38 See, in particular, Mark Neocleous, *Imagining the State* (Maidenhead: Open University Press, 2003).

39 Alasdair MacIntyre, *After Virtue* (London: Duckworth, 1979); Charles Taylor, *Sources of the Self* (Cambridge, MA: Harvard University Press, 1989); Michael Sandel, *Liberalism and the Limits of Justice* (New York and Cambridge: Cam-bridge University Press, 1982); and Michael Walzer, *Spheres of Justice* (Oxford: Martin Robertson, 1983).

40 Robert Bellah et al., *Habits of the Heart: Individualism and Commitment in American Life* (Berkeley, CA: University of California Press, 1986); *The Good Society* (New York: Knopf, 1991).

41 See the journal founded by Etzioni and others, *The Responsive Community*.

42 Cris Shore, "Community," in William Outhwaite (ed.), *The Blackwell Dic-tionary of Modern Social Thought* (Oxford: Blackwell, 2003), pp. 101–2.

43 Nikolas Rose, "'The Death of the Social?' Re-figuring the Territory of Government," *Economy and Society* 25: 3 (1996), pp. 327–56. See also Rose's recent interview (discussed in more detail in Chapter 6 in this volume), in Nicholas Gane (ed.), *The Future of Social Theory* (London: Continuum, 2004), Chapter 9.

44 "The Death of the Social?," p. 342.

45 Ibid., p. 347.

46 Ibid., p. 336. See also the discussion of these issues in Chapter 6, pp. 92–3.

47 For an excellent overview, see Gerard Delanty, *Community* (London: Routledge, 2003. As Delanty notes there (pp. 113–20), recent critics of "community"

include Habermas, Touraine and Bauman. Conversely, "community" is some-times presented as a successor to "society," as in Jean-Luc Nancy's political philosophy: "community . . . is what happens to us . . . in the wake of society" (Nancy, *The Inoperative Community*, Minneapolis: University of Minnesota Press, 1991), p. 11. For a more positive view, see Paul Hopper, *Rebuilding Communities in an Age of Individualism* (Aldershot: Ashgate, 2005).

48 As Eric Hobsbawm put it in *The Age of Extremes* (London: Abacus, 1995), p. 428: "Never was the word 'community' used more indiscriminately and emptily than in the decades when communities in the sociological sense became hard to find in real life."

49 There is a parallel in the way in which the "mass society" theory of the mid-twentieth century moved from claims about the atomization of modern societies to assertions about the vulnerability of their members to the appeal of charismatic movements. What is often taken as a contradiction in mass society theory (which I do not want to defend here, or indeed at all), might be better understood as a description of a contradictory process of this kind. Accounts of totalitarian and post-totalitarian state socialist societies, whether or not they draw on mass society theory, tend similarly to oscillate between an emphasis on collectivism, social pressure, groupthink and surveillance and the suggestion, for which there is also good evidence, that these were essen-tially fragmented and atomized societies.

Chapter 3 Postmodernism

1 J.-F. Lyotard, *Le postmoderne expliqué aux enfants* (Paris: Gallilée, 1986), p. 38. Translated as *The Post Modern Explained to Children* (London: Turnaround, 1992), p. 30.

2 J.-F. Lyotard, *La Condition postmoderne: rapport sur le savoir* (Paris: Minuit, 1979). *The Postmodern Condition: A Report on Knowledge*, trans. Geoff Bennington and Brian Massumi (Minneapolis, MN: University of Minnesota Press, 1984), p. 14.

3 Baudrillard rejects the label (see Mike Gane, *Baudrillard: Critical and Fatal Theory* (London: Routledge, 1991), Chapter 3; also Paul Hegarty, *Jean Baudrillard: Live Theory* (London: Continuum, 2004), Introduction), but it still seems to me the most appropriate one for his work. It is true that he does not celebrate postmodernity, but that would be true of many other postmodern thinkers (see below). His critique of Foucault can be found in his *Oublier Foucault* (Paris: Galilée, 1977) and in his *Cool Memories* (London: Verso, 1990), pp. 157–61.

4 Chris Rojek and Bryan Turner, *Forget Baudrillard* (London: Routledge, 1993), p. xiv.

5   P.M. Rosenau, *Post-Modernism and the Social Sciences* (Princeton, NJ: Princeton University Press, 1992). One of Rosenau's section headings (ibid., p. 71) aptly captures the skeptical motif: "Post-Modern Social Science – Without History, on New Time, Drifting in Space."

6   Maffesoli, *The Shadow of Dionysus* (Paris: Méridiens, 1982. Tr. Albany: SUNY Press, 1993). *The Times of the Tribes* (Paris: Méridiens, 1988).

7   Jean Baudrillard, *A l'ombre des majorités silencieuses: La fin du social* (Paris: Denoël-Gonthier, 1982), p. 71. Translated as *In the Shadow of the Silent Majorities* (New York: Semiotext(e), 1983), pp. 67–8.

8   Ibid., p. 9; trans., p. 4.

9   Ibid., p. 72; trans., p. 68.

10 Ibid., p. 87; trans., p. 83.

11 Ibid., p. 80; trans., p. 76.

12 Ibid., p. 76, n. 1; trans., p. 90.

13 Ibid., p. 78; trans., p. 74.

14 Ibid., p. 74, n. 1; trans., p. 90.

15 It is worth noting that Lyotard (trans., p. 15) explicitly rejects Baudrillard's claims:

> The breaking up of the grand Narratives . . . leads to what some authors analyze in terms of the dissolution of the social bond and the disintegration of social aggregates into a mass of individual atoms thrown into the absurdity of Brownian motion. Nothing of the kind is happening: this point of view, it seems to me, is haunted by the paradisiac representation of a lost "organic" society.

16 Gilles Lipovetsky, *L'ère du vide: essais sur l'individualisme contemporain* (Paris: Gallimard, 1983), pp. 15–16.

17 Ibid., p. 61.

18 Ibid., p. 7.

19 *La Connaissance ordinaire: Précis de sociologie compréhensive* (Paris: Méridiens, 1985), p. 186. Trans. as *Ordinary Knowledge* (Cambridge: Polity, 1996).

20 Ibid., p. 180.

21 Bryan Turner, "Baudrillard for Sociologists," in Chris Rojek and Bryan S. Turner, *Forget Baudrillard?* (London: Routledge, 1993), p. 71; G. Stauth and B.S. Turner, *Nietzsche's Dance: Resentment, Reciprocity and Distance in Social Life* (Oxford: Blackwell, 1988), p. 53. See also M. Gane, *Baudrillard: Critical and Fatal Theory* (London: Routledge, 1991), p. 48.

22 Kroker, in Arthur Kroker and David Crook, *The Postmodern Scene: Excremental Culture and Hyper-aesthetics* (Basingstoke: Macmillan Education, 1988), p. 188.

23 "Baudrillard for Sociologists," p. 73.

24 Ibid., p. 84.

25 Stauth and Turner, *Nietzsche's Dance*, p. 3. Since the publication of their book, this has indeed happened, in at least three forms, though none of them, as it happens, particularly influenced by Nietzsche. I refer in particular to Axel Honneth's development of the Hegelian motif of recognition in *The Struggle for Recognition* (Frankfurt: Suhrkamp, 1992; Cambridge: Polity, 1995) and to the reception, by Bauman and others, of Emmanuel Levinas' ethical theory. Most recently, Nathalie Karagiannis and Peter Wagner have been developing a model of synagonism, a kind of cooperative competition; see Karagiannis and Wagner, "Rethinking the Social and the Political: Towards a Theory of Synagonism," *Journal of Political Philosophy* (13: 3 (Sept 2005, pp. 235–262).

26 Jean Baudrillard, *A l'ombre des majorités silencieuses: La fin du social* (Paris: Denoël-Gonthier, 1982), p. 12. Trans., pp. 6–7.

27 Michel Freitag, *L'oubli de la société* (Rennes: Presses Universitaires de Rennes 2002), p. 45.

28 Ibid., p. 86.

29 Zygmunt Bauman, *Society under Siege* (Cambridge: Polity, 2002), pp. 44–5.

30 Richard Sennett, *Corrosion of Character: The Personal Consequences of Work in the New Capitalism* (New York: W.W. Norton, 1998), p. 51. Cf. Bauman, *Society Under Siege*, p. 38.

31 Daniel Cohen, *Nos temps modernes* (Paris: Flammarion, 1999), p. 60. Cohen quotes a book by Alain Ehrenberg, *La fatigue d'être soi* (Paris: Odile Jacob, 1998) which suggests that the majority of mental illnesses are now made up of depressions related to performance anxiety.

32 Ibid., p. 56. As Bauman notes, Luc Boltanski and Ève Chiapello, in *Le nouvel esprit du capitalisme* (Paris: Gallimard, 1999), p. 151, similarly stress the pre-dominance of *savoir-être* over *savoir-faire*.

33 Bauman, *Society under Siege*, p. 49.

34 Ibid., p. 43.

35 Or, as my deconstructionist and anti-foundationalist friends sometimes say, "what we used to call postmodernism." I have discussed these issues at more length in "The Myth of Modernist Method," *European Journal of Social Theory* 1: 2 (Feb. 1999), pp. 5–25.

36 Lyotard, *Le postmoderne expliqué aux enfants*, trans. p. 30. There was, of course, a performative contradiction in Lyotard's analysis, in that his story was itself a "grand narrative" of the kind whose alleged end he had recorded.

37 This gave it a certain appeal in post-communist Europe in the late 1980s and 1990s, reinforced by a sense of the factitious and absurd character of many of the economic and financial operations taking place there. For a fuller discussion, see William Outhwaite and Larry Ray, *Social Theory and Postcommunism* (Oxford: Blackwell, 2005), Chapter 5.

38 This term seems to have been invented in the USA as a label for various types of French theory with intrinsically little in common except that their inventors had once been thought of, though generally not by themselves, as structuralists. Bourdieu, whose thinking really did emerge from a positive critique of structural anthropology, was not, of course, a post-structuralist in this sense.

39 My own inclination is to minimize the alleged gap between description and explanation. See my article, "Hermeneutic and Phenomenological Approaches," in Mark Risjord and Stephen Turner (eds.), *Handbook of the Philosophy of Sociology and Anthropology* (Oxford: Elsevier, 2005).

40 Durkheim, *Règles*, p. 144; *Rules* (1982), p. 163.

41 Cf. Stepan Mestrovic, *Émile Durkheim and the Reformulation of Sociology* (Lanham, MD: Rowman and Littlefield, 1993).

42 J. Margolis, "Postscript on Modernism and Postmodernism, Both," *Theory, Culture & Society* 6: 1 (1989), pp. 5–30.

43 Ali Rattansi, "Just Framing: Ethnicities and Racisms in a 'Postmodern' Framework," in Linda Nicholson and Steve Seidman (eds.), *Social Postmodernism: Beyond Identity Politics* (Cambridge: Cambridge University Press), p. 250.

44 Ibid., pp. 34–5.

45 Rob Stones, *Sociological Reasoning: Towards a Past-Modern Sociology* (Basingstoke: Macmillan, 1996).

46 Claus Offe, *Disorganized Capitalism* (Cambridge: Polity, 1985); Alain Touraine, *Critique of Modernity* (Oxford: Blackwell, 1995); Ulrich Beck, *The Risk Society: Towards a New Modernity* (London: Sage, 1992); Peter Wagner, *A Sociology of Modernity: Liberty and Discipline* (London: Routledge, 1994). Each of these authors has continued these reflections in subsequent works.

47 Anton Zijderveld, *The Abstract Society* (London: Allen Lane, 1972), pp. 48ff.

48 I am of course borrowing the title of Dipesh Chakrabarty's book, though in the sense which he distinguishes from the one he intends in the book. "*Provincializing Europe* is not a book about the region of the world we call Europe. That world, one could say, has already been provincialized by history itself" (*Provincializing Europe*, Princeton, NJ: Princeton University Press, 2002), p. 3.

49 Peter Osborne, in his brilliant book *The Politics of Time: Modernity and Avant-Garde* (London: Verso, 1995), suggests that Marxism, by locating the contrast between traditional and modern in a succession of modes of production, escapes and challenges what he calls "the complacency of the sociological category of modernity" (ibid., p. 2), as do later theories of postmodernity. (See below, p. 142, n. 4). I have suggested elsewhere that in retrospect the mid-twentieth century should probably be seen as no less exceptional in its social thought than it was in its triumphant capitalism in the 30 years from the end of World War II to the mid-1970s (*les trente glorieuses*). See my "The Myth of Modernist Method."

Chapter 4 Globalization

1 See, for instance, from *The Communist Manifesto*, p. 83: "The bourgeoisie has, through its exploitation of the world market, given a cosmopolitan character to production and consumption in every country."

2 Marshall McLuhan, *The Gutenberg Galaxy* (London: Routledge, 1962).

3 Immanuel Wallerstein, *The Modern World System* (New York: Academic Press, 1974).

4 Martin Albrow and Elizabeth King, in *Globalization, Knowledge and Society* (London: Sage, 1990), reprint articles from the first six years of the International Sociological Association's journal *International Sociology* which illustrate the emergence of a concern with globalization from earlier phases of sociology: Albrow characterizes these as *universalism* (in classical sociology), the *national sociologies* of the early twentieth century, *internationalization* (after World War II) and *indigenization* (a response from the "Third World" to the dominance of "Western" categories of theorizing). See the discussion of Wallerstein, below.

5 On the relation between globalization and the end of communism and its aftermath, see W. Outhwaite and L. Ray, *Social Theory and Postcommunism* (Oxford: Blackwell, 2005), especially Chapter 6.

6 Often, of course, over-stated. For critiques of hyper-globalist overstatement, see, in particular, the work of Linda Weiss, *The Myth of the Powerless State: Governing the Economy in a Global Era* (Cambridge: Polity, 1998); also Daniel Chernilo, "Sociology and the Nation-State," unpublished PhD thesis, University of Warwick, 2004, p. 42. See also Chernilo, "Social Theory's Methodological Nationalism: Myth and Reality" (*European Journal of Social Theory* forthcoming). Some critics, of course, reject the very concept of globalization; see, in particular, Paul Hirst and Grahame Thompson, *Globalization in Question* (Cambridge: Polity, 1996); and Justin Rosenberg, *The Follies of Globalisation Theory* (London: Verso, 2000).

7 Immanuel Wallerstein "Societal Development, or Development of the World-System?" reprinted in Albrow and King (eds.), *Globalization, Knowledge and Society*, pp. 157–71, quote from p. 163.

8 Ibid., p. 163.

9 Ibid., p. 165.

10 Ibid., p. 166. See also Wallerstein's postface to the second French edition of *Historical Capitalism*: "Globalisation is not new."

11 See, for example, Dipesh Chakrabarty, *Provincializing Europe* (Princeton, NJ: Princeton University Press, 2000); Gurminder Bhambra, "Contesting Modernity," unpublished PhD thesis, University of Sussex (publication forthcoming).

12 *The Global Age* (Cambridge: Polity, 1996), p. 19.

13 Ibid., p. 47.

14 Ibid., p. 65.

15 *Sociology Beyond Societies* (London: Routledge, 2000), pp. 32–3.

16 Outhwaite and Ray, *Social Theory*, pp. 198–9.

17 Albrow, *The Global Age*, p. 6.

18 Ibid., Chapter 7, *passim.* Albrow's analysis here converges with theories of reflexive modernity and communicatively negotiated social relations.

19 Ibid., p. 167, n. 3, p. 217.

20 Ibid., Chapter 8.

21 Martin Shaw, *Theory of the Global State* (Cambridge: Cambridge University Press, 2000).

22 Ibid., pp. 175–6.

23 "Globalization or World Society: How to Conceive of Modern Society," *International Review of Sociology* 7: 1 (March 1997), pp. 67–80; quote, p. 72. See also his major work of the same year, *Die Gesellschaft der Gesellschaft* (Frankfurt: Suhrkamp, 1997), especially Chapter 1, section X, pp. 145–71. As Luhmann notes, pp. 158–9, sociologists have mostly resisted the idea of conceptualizing the global system as a society, tending to assume that a world society does not yet exist.

24 Ibid., p. 67.

25 It may, however, be the case, as Beck suggests in *Der kosmopolitischer Blick* (Frankfurt: Suhrkamp, 2004), p. 45, n. 7, that Luhmann's system model remains inextricably bound up with a nation-state framework.

26 I am not of course denying the point, made notably by Durkheim in his theory of religion, that members' conceptions of society typically include an idealized image of it. Nor do I deny the point, made in a rather different way by Ulrich Beck, that a preoccupation with distributional inequality characteristic of classical industrial societies has been in part supplanted by concern with (other types of) risk.

27 Luhmann, "Globalization or World Society," p. 73.

28 See also the more empirically oriented work of Peter Heintz and others in Zürich and the group around John Meyer at Stanford. For useful overviews, see the work of Rudolf Stichweh.

29 When a writer such as Christopher Chase-Dunn defines a world-system in terms of "intersocietal and trans-societal relations" (*Global Formation: Structures of the World-Economy*, Oxford: Blackwell, 1989), p. 1, it may not be so significant, *pace* Luhmann (*Gesellschaft der Gesellschaft*, p. 159, n. 215), that he does not make explicit reference to the concept of society.

30 Rudolf Stichweh, "Differenz und Integration in der Weltgesellschaft," reprinted in Stichweh, *Die Weltgesellschaft* (Frankfurt: Suhrkamp, 2000), p. 31.

31 For a skeptical view, see Friedrich Kratochwil, "Global Governance and the emergence of 'world society'" (in Peter Wagner (ed.), *The Languages of Civil Society* (Oxford: Berghahn), forthcoming).

Chapter 5 Modernity and Society

1 François Dubet and Danilo Martuccelli, *Dans quelle société vivons-nous?* (Paris: Seuil, 1998), p. 22.

2 Although Alain Touraine, the first of this group of thinkers, only later wrote explicitly about modernity (1992), his earlier concept of historicity, meaning the capacity of a society to shape itself, is a key element of his and others' later theories of modernity as they developed in the 1980s.

3 Tocqueville leaves us with, as well as his often neglected historical and sociological observations, the image of him leading his household from his chateau near Cherbourg to the polling station opened up to universal male suffrage in 1848.

4 Marx and Engels, *The Manifesto of the Communist Party* (1848) (London: Penguin, 1967). Peter Osborne, as noted earlier, suggests that Marxism, by locating the contrast between traditional and modern in a succession of modes of production, escapes and challenges what he calls "the complacency of the sociological category of modernity" (*The Politics of Time: Modernity and Avant-Garde*, London: Verso, 1995, p. 2), as do later theories of postmodernity. Without wishing to deny the differences between revolutionary Marxism and most other strands of social theory, I am not sure that this is one of them. Osborne's question (ibid., p. 3) is, however, an important one:

> whether the relocation of the sociological conception of modernity within the developmental perspective of historical materialism affects its temporal structure as a category of historical periodization, or whether it just gives it a new, changing historical content. Is there a new conception of historical time implicit in the developmental perspective of a materialist conception of history?

At all events, as Osborne points out, later Marxists have mostly ignored this possibility.

5 See, for example, Wallerstein's reference to it in the previous chapter.

6 *The Protestant Ethic and the Spirit of Capitalism* (1904/5), trans. Stephen Kalberg (Los Angeles: Roxbury, 2001), p. 122.

7 Ibid., p. 160.

8 Emile Durkheim, *The Elementary Forms of Religious Life* (London: Free Press, 1995), p. 106.

9 Ibid., p. 118.

142

10 Ibid., p. 123.

11 See, for example, Norbert Elias, *The Society of Individuals*, ed. Michael Schröter (Oxford: Blackwell, 1991) and Charles Taylor's *Modern Social Imaginaries* (Durham, NC: Duke University Press, 2004), discussed below.

12 On the former issue see, for example, Dipesh Chakrabarty, *Provincializing Europe* (Princeton, NJ: Princeton University Press, 2000) and Gurminder Bhambra, "Contesting Modernity" (forthcoming). I have tried to do justice to these criticisms in my essay on "European Transformations," forthcoming in Gerard Delanty (ed.), *Handbook of Contemporary European Social Theory* (London: Sage, 2005) and in a forthcoming book on European society and culture. On the latter issue, Barrington Moore, in his *Injustice: Reflections on the Causes of Human Misery* (London: Allen Lane, 1972) showed, for example, how little there was of an urban industrial proletariat at the time Marx and Engels appealed to it. Bruno Latour, in *We Have Never Been Modern* (Cambridge, MA: Harvard University Press, 1993) has similarly questioned the extent to which the "scientific revolution" and the Enlightenment were diffused and internalized.

13 Norbert Elias, "The Retreat of Sociologists into the Present," *Theory, Culture & Society*, 4: 2–3 (June 1987), pp. 223–47.

14 Anthony Giddens, "Four Myths in the History of Social Thought," *Economy and Society*, 1, 1972, pp. 357ff. Reprinted in Giddens, *Studies in Social and Political Theory* (London: Hutchinson, 1977).

15 Charles Taylor, *Modern Social Imaginaries*, p. 23.

16 Ibid., p. 31. As Baczko puts it, in *Les imaginaires sociaux* (Paris: Payot, 1984), p. 18, these representations include "ideas, rituals and forms of action. Representations, and not *reflections* of a 'reality' existing outside them . . . How could one separate . . . the actors and their acts from the ideas/images which they give of themselves and their adversaries?" As Baczko notes (ibid., pp. 31–2), the term "social" refers both to the object of the representations (society or social relations) and to their collective character.

17 Taylor, *Modern Social Imaginaries*, p. 64. One would clearly have to qualify and elaborate this simple contrast in relation to, for example, self-conceptions in classical Europe in the "pre-modern" era, and the modulations of class, culture and gender in the "modern." I believe, however, that much of it would survive these operations. The multiple modernities of, for example, East Asia in the twentieth century and into the present century seem to me to confirm this. See, in particular, the work of Shmuel Eisenstadt (*Comparative Civilizations and Multiple Modernities*, Leiden: Brill, 2003); also Gerard Delanty's *Modernity and Postmodernity* (London: Sage, 2000) and his "Modernity and the Escape from Eurocentrism," in G. Delanty (ed.), *Handbook of Contemporary European Social Theory* (London: Sage, 2005).

18 Taylor, *Modern Social Imaginaries*, p. 77.

19 Giddens, *Modernity and Self-Identity* (Cambridge: Polity, 1991), p. 91. I have discussed this more fully in relation to Andrew Collier's work in a contribution to his Festschrift: "Intentional and Reflexive Objectivity: Some Reflections," in Margaret Archer and William Outhwaite (eds.), *Defending Objectivity* (London: Routledge, 2003).

20 *Between Facts and Norms* (Cambridge: Polity, 1996).

21 Taylor, *Modern Social Imaginaries*, p. 165.

22 Raymond Boudon, *Effets pervers et ordre social* (Paris: Presses Universitaires de France, 1977).

23 David Lockwood, "Social Integration and System Integration," in G.K. Zollschan and W. Hirsch (eds.), *Explorations in Social Change* (London: Routledge, 1964). For a discussion which relates Lockwood's distinction to more recent accounts of agency and structure, see Margaret Archer, "Social Integration and System Integration: Developing the Distinction," *Sociology* 30, 4, 1996, pp. 679–99.

24 Talcott Parsons, *The Structure of Social Action* (New York: Free Press, 1968), pp. 89–94.

25 Lockwood, "Social Integration," p. 245.

26 The line between Lukács's *History and Class Consciousness*, published in 1923 (trans. London: Merlin Press, 1971) and the work of what came to be called the Frankfurt School less than a decade later is one place where one could locate this watershed. Although Lukács's book was published in the aftermath of the failed Marxist revolutions of 1918, his tone remains optimistic.

27 *Sociologie de l'action* (Paris: Seuil, 1965), p. 53.

28 "The Useless Idea of Society" (1980), "Putting an End to the Idea of Society" (1980), "Sociology Without Society" (1981), "Is Sociology Still the Study of Society?" (1987, trans. 1989), and more recently "Culture Without Society" (1998), "From Understanding Society to Discovering the Subject" (2001), and "Sociology without Societies" (2003). Full details are given in the Bibliography.

29 Touraine, "Le traitement de la société globale dans la sociologie américaine contemporaine," *Cahiers Internationaux de Sociologie*, 16, 1954, p. 136.

30 *Sociologie de l'action*, p. 99.

31 Ibid., p. 106.

32 Ibid., p. 89. (There are of course parallels here with Giddens' attempt to bridge these gaps.)

33 *La Société invisible* (Paris: Seuil, 1977), p. 7; cf. *Critique de la modernité* (Paris: Fayard, 1992), p. 209.

34 *La Société invisible*, p. 7.

35 Ibid., p. 74. The echo of Pierre Clastres's title, *Society against the State* (Paris: Minuit, 1974; trans. Oxford: Blackwell, 1977) may or may not be intended.

36 Touraine, *Le retour de l'acteur* (Paris: Seuil, 1984), p. 27.
37 *La Société invisible*, pp. 187–9; cf. *Le retour*, pp. 29–31.
38 *Le retour*, p. 29.
39 Ibid., p. 49.
40 Ibid., p. 42.
41 Ibid., p. 84.
42 *Critique de la modernité*, p. 332.
43 *Le retour de l'acteur*, p. 330.
44 Ibid., pp. 335–6.
45 Ibid., p. 338.
46 Touraine (1999), p. 7.
47 Jon Clark and Marco Diani (eds.), *Alain Touraine* (London: Falmer Press, 1996).
48 The book is dedicated to him.
49 *Dans quelle société vivons-nous?* (Paris: Seuil, 1998), p. 296, my translation.
50 Ibid., p. 65. They aim, then, to avoid the extreme of a fascination with the void (Lipovetsky, Baudrillard).
51 Ibid., p. 299.
52 Ibid., p. 300.
53 The former term was imported from France into academic discussion in the UK and then into public policy with the coming to power in 1997 of the Blair government, which rapidly set up a Social Exclusion Unit. Precarity has not yet made its way into UK usage, where it is even more needed, in a context of poorly regulated labour markets and a ruthless "hire and fire" managerial culture.
54 Dubet and Martuccelli, *Dans quelle société vivons-nous?*, p. 119.
55 Ibid., p. 278.
56 Ibid., p. 170. Some theorists, they note, like Luhmann, see this as an additional reason in favor of their preferred models of system integration.
57 Ibid., p. 171.
58 Ibid., p. 294.
59 Ibid., p. 299.
60 See, for example, pp. 12 and 295.
61 Peter Wagner, *A History and Theory of the Social Sciences* (London: Sage, 2001), p. 131.
62 Quoted by Lewis Coser, *Georg Simmel* (Englewood Cliffs, NJ: Prentice-Hall, 1965), p. 39.
63 Thomas Paine, *Common Sense* (ed. I. Kramnick, Harmondsworth: Penguin, 1776), p. 65.
64 Pierre Clastres, *La société contre l'état*. Trans. as *Society against the State*.
65 The title of an earlier version of the chapter referred to here.

145

66 Ibid., p. 144.
67 Ibid., p. 144.
68 Ibid., p. 145.

Chapter 6 Towards a Synthesis? Theory and Metatheory

1 (Leeds: Leeds Books, 1975); 2nd edn. (Brighton: Harvester, 1978).
2 Reprinted in Kurt Wolff (ed.), *Georg Simmel* (Columbus, OH: Ohio University Press 1959), p. 338.
3 See Karin Schrader-Klebert, "Der Begriff der Gesellschaft als regulative Idee: Zur transzendentalen Begründung der Soziologie bei Georg Simmel," *Soziale Welt* 19: 2 (1968), pp. 97–118.
4 Wolff, *Georg Simmel*, p. 340; see also David Frisby, *Georg Simmel* (revised edition, London: Routledge 2002, pp. 120–3). Alternatively, as Frisby notes (p. 123), one can read Simmel's analysis phenomenologically, as John O'Neill does in his *Sociology as a Skin Trade* (London, Heinemann, 1972), pp. 167–76.
5 Daniel Chernilo, unpublished PhD thesis, University of Warwick, 2004, p. 42. See also Chernilo, "Social Theory's Methodological Nationalism: Myth and Reality" (forthcoming).
6 Max Adler, "Die Staatsauffassung des Marxismus," in *Marx-Studien*, vol. IV, eds M.A. Hilferding and R. Hilferding (Vienna, 1922, reprinted Darmstadt: Wissenschaftliche Buchgesellschaft, 1973).
7 See Frisby, *Simmel*, pp. 122–3. As Frisby's book (especially Chapter 3) makes clear, this text comes more or less in the middle of a long series of reflections on the foundations of sociology. See also Uta Gerhardt, *Rollenanalyse als kritische Soziologie* (Neuwied and Berlin: Luchterhand, 1971), pp. 27–40.
8 Giambattista Vico, in his *Scienza Nuova* of 1725, suggested that human beings could understand the human world because they had created it: only God could have that kind of understanding of the natural world. This is usually, and rightly, taken to be the origin of German idealism and the division between the world of nature and of mind or spirit; it can also, however, be read in this more materialist way.
9 Alfred Schmidt, *The Concept of Nature in Marx* (London: New Left Books, 1971). See also Schmidt (ed.), *Beiträge zur marxistischen Erkenntnistheorie* (Frankfurt: Suhrkamp, 1969).
10 This is clearly one way of reading the quotation above, p. 76.
11 Adler suggests that Simmel was diverted from epistemology to a focus on the "psychological preconditions of human interaction" (*Das Rätsel der Gesellschaft: Zur erkenntniskritischen Grundlegung der Sozialwissenschaft* (Vienna: Saturn-Verlag, 1936), p. 205.

12 See note 4, above.

13 *The Sociology of Georg Simmel*, ed. K. Wolff (Chicago: Free Press, 1950), pp. 10ff.

14 (Leipzig: Duncker & Humblot, 1890), p. 10.

15 Wolff, *The Sociology of Georg Simmel*, pp. 11ff.

16 *Soziologische Vorlesungen von Georg Simmel*, Ed. Society for Social Research (Chicago: University of Chicago Press, 1931), p. 4.

17 Schrader-Klebert, "Der Begriff," p. 107.

18 "The Problem of Society," in K. Wolff (ed.), *The Sociology of Georg Simmel*, p. 316.

19 See n. 34, p. 130, above.

20 "My Relation to Sociology," in Ferdinand Tönnies, *On Sociology: Pure, Applied and Empirical* (Chicago: University of Chicago Press, 1971), p. 10.

21 Ibid., p. 6.

22 "The Psychological Import of the Human Group," cited by Walter Buckley, *Sociology and Modern Systems Theory* (Englewood Cliffs, NJ: Prentice-Hall, 1967), pp. 21ff.

23 Schutz, *The Phenomenology of the Social World* (London: Heinemann, 1972), p. 4.

24 *The Social Construction of Reality* (Harmondsworth: Penguin, 1966), p. 30.

25 Max Adler, *Die Staatsauffassung des Marxismus* (Darmstadt: Wissenschaftliche Buchgesellschaft, 1973), trans. in Tom Bottomore and Patrick Goode (eds.), *Austro-Marxism* (Oxford: Clarendon Press, 1978).

26 "Vorlesung zur Einleitung in die Soziologie" (Frankfurt: Junius, 1973), p. 112.

27 Institut für Sozialforschung, *Soziologische Exkurse* (Frankfurt: 1956), p. 43. Trans. as Institute for Social Research, *Aspects of Sociology* (London: Heinemann, 1973). One of Adorno's recent biographers, Stefan Müller-Doohm, tells us that he kept this quotation above his desk while working on the biography (*Adorno: Eine Biographie* (Frankfurt: Suhrkamp, 2003), p. 12.

28 *The Sociology of Georg Simmel*, p. 10. Adorno, *Vorlesung*.

29 Simmel, "Society," *Gesammelte Schriften*, vol. 8 (trans. in *Salmagundi* 11–12 (fall-winter 1969–70), pp. 144–3). Cf. Adorno, *Gesammelte Schriften*, vol. 8, pp. 238ff.; "Notiz über sozialwissenchaftlicher Objektivität."

30 *Vorlesung*, pp. 33ff; "Society," pp. 148ff.

31 *The Positivist Dispute in German Sociology*, pp. 79ff.

32 *Vorlesung*, pp. 156ff.

33 See, in particular, "Sociology and Psychology," *New Left Review* 46–47, 1967/8.

34 *New Left Review* 46, p. 68.

35 Ibid., pp. 68–9.

36 Ibid., p. 77.

37 Ibid., p. 70.

38 Ibid., p. 73.

39 "Society," pp. 146ff.

40 Adorno et al., *The Positivist Dispute in German Sociology* (London: Heinemann, 1976), p. 74.

41 See Adorno's introduction to the German edition of Durkheim's *Sociology and Philosophy*, in Adorno, *Gesammelte Schriften*, vol. 8, especially pp. 250ff.

42 *Vorlesung*, p. 92.

43 "Society," p. 146.

44 Adorno, *Gesammelte Schriften*, vol. 8, pp. 184ff. ("Anmerkungen zum sozialen Konflikt Heute").

45 See, for example, his *Dissonanzen* (4th edn., Göttingen: Vandenhoeck and Ruprecht, 1969), pp. 18ff.

46 *Aspects of Sociology*, p. 121.

47 Adorno, "A European Scholar in America," in D. Fleming and B. Bailyn (eds), *The Intellectual Migration* (Cambridge, MA: Harvard University Press, 1969), p. 346.

48 I am referring here to Bhaskar's earlier work, rather than to the more complex dialectical models which he has subsequently developed. These are, however, I believe, compatible with what is discussed here, though they go beyond it in all sorts of ways.

49 Cf. Bhaskar, *The Possibility of Naturalism*, pp. 18ff.

50 Ibid., p. 182.

51 For a recent lively exchange between the two, see "How to Change Reality: Story Versus Structure," in José López and Garry Potter (eds.), *After Postmodernism: An Introduction to Critical Realism* (London: Athlone, 2001).

52 *Naturalism*, p. 31.

53 Ibid., pp. 42ff.

54 *The Social Construction of Reality*, p. 30.

55 *Naturalism*, p. 42.

56 Ibid., p. 43.

57 Ibid., p. 42.

58 Ibid., pp. 34ff.

59 Ibid., p. 52.

60 Anthony Giddens, *The Constitution of Society* (Cambridge: Polity, 1984), p. xxi. See also Giddens' diagram on p. 25 and his gloss on the same page: "According to the notion of the duality of structure, the structural properties of social systems are both medium and outcome of the practices they recursively organise."

61 Ibid., pp. xxvi–xxvii; cf. pp. 163–8. Giddens goes on to stress the importance of what he calls "time-space edges" and "intersocietal systems."

62 Margaret Archer, *Realist Social Theory: The Morphogenetic Approach* (Cambridge: Cambridge University Press, 1995), p. 11.

63 Ibid., see the diagram on p. 157. "The Elisionists," she writes [i.e. Giddens and those following his concept of structuration], "deliberately turn their backs upon any autonomous features which could pertain independently to either 'structure' or 'agency'."

64 See, for example, *Culture and Agency* (Cambridge: Cambridge University Press, 1988), p. 305.

65 Realists, in other words, are unhappy to use Bourdieu's get-out clause that all claims about structural properties in the social sciences should be preceded with the health warning "everything happens as if . . .".

66 See the splendid discussion in *Realist Social Theory*, Chapter 2.

67 The subtitle of *The Possibility of Naturalism*.

68 In a much earlier discussion of these issues at the time when these contributions were being formulated, and on which I have drawn from time to time here, I wrote: "How far such work retains the concept of society in a prominent position is a matter of secondary importance, so long as sociologists continue to do justice to the themes with which it has always been inextricably associated." (*Concept Formation in Social Science*, 1983, p. 154). In the present work it is of course difficult to take quite such a laid-back position, but I remain committed to it – with, of course, the qualification that the secondary is not unimportant, except with reference to the primary.

69 See, in particular, Sayer, *Realism and Social Science* (London: Sage, 2000).

70 See, in particular, Berth Danermark et al., *Explaining Society* (London: Routledge, 2002). Charles Crothers' *Social Structure* (London: Routledge, 1996) is also influenced by realism.

71 The classic example is of course the USA, which has had strong and active trade unions with the absence of class consciousness and explicitly class-based politics in the European sense.

72 *The Future of Social Theory* (London and New York: Continuum, 2004), p. 2.

73 Bauman, in ibid., p. 21.

74 Ibid., p. 33. Compare Sassen's metaphor referred to above.

75 Urry, in ibid., p. 109.

76 Donzelot, *La police des familles* (Paris: Minuit, 1977), trans. as *The Policing of Families* (London: Hutchinson, 1980); *L'invention du social* (Paris: Fayard, 1984).

77 Rose, in Gane, *The Future of Social Theory*, p. 179.

78 Ibid., p. 181.

79 According to Latour, in Gane:

> The notion of society is the last remnant of transcendence in social sciences that do not care for religion . . . It does nothing but reassures, gives moral comfort, and allows the sociologist to have an overview. And that is why I am fighting it. (ibid., pp. 84–5)

80 Ibid., p. 83.

81 Latour's classic ethnographic study written with Steve Woolgar, *Laboratory Life: The Social Construction of Scientific Facts* (London: Sage, 1979), especially Chapter 2, illustrates this neatly, especially in the powerful image of the transformation of the bits and pieces on the scientist's desk (drafts, photocopies, scraps of paper, old plane tickets etc) into the final product, the research paper.

82 Benton presents some of these arguments briefly in "Why are Sociologists Naturophobes?" in López and Potter (eds.), *After Postmodernism* (London: Athlone, 2001), Chapter 9, pp. 133–45.

83 Gane, *The Future of Society*, pp. 154–5.

84 See, for example, his "Beyond Class and Status," in Volker Meja, Dieter Misgeld and Nico Stehr (eds.), *Modern German Sociology* (New York: Columbia University Press, 1987).

Chapter 7 Society Lite? Theories of Civil Society

1 See Peter Hallberg, *The Return of Aristotle* (2 vols.), forthcoming. I am indebted to Peter Hallberg and Björn Wittrock for the draft presented to the CiSoNet conference at EUI, Florence, November 2003.

2 Maurizio Viroli, "Machiavelli and the Republican Idea of Politics," in Gisela Bock, Quentin Skinner and Maurizio Viroli (eds.), *Machiavelli and Republicanism* (Cambridge: Cambridge University Press, 1990), p. 147.

3 *Civil Society and Political Theory* (Cambridge, MA: MIT Press, 1992). See also Jean Cohen, *Class and Civil Society* (Oxford: Martin Robertson, 1983); John Keane (ed.) *Civil Society and the State: New European Perspectives* (London: Verso, 1988); Krishan Kumar, "Civil Society," in K. Kumar, *1989: Revolutionary Ideas and Ideals* (Minneapolis: Minnesota University Press, 2001); Sudipta Kaviraj and Sunil Khilnani (eds.), *Civil Society: History and Possibilities* (Cambridge: Cambridge University Press, 2001).

4 Tönnies is interesting in this connection, in that his ideal-typical dichotomy between *Gemeinschaft* and *Gesellschaft* immediately raises questions about *Gesellschaft*-type associations displaying solidarity of a kind otherwise associated with *Gemeinschaft*. As Kaviraj puts it, "It has been argued that the proper working of a modern constitutional state requires a distinction not merely between state and other organizations in society, but the sphere of non-state organizations being governed by *Gesellschaft*-like principles." (Kaviraj, "In Search of Civil Society," in Sudipta Kaviraj and Sunil Khilnani (eds.), *Civil Society: History and Possibilities* (Cambridge: Cambridge University Press, 2001).

Herman Schmalenbach, in his book *Der Bund*, oddly translated as *Communion* (Chicago: University of Chicago Press, 1977), made an important contribution to the conceptualization of political and other associations of this kind.

5 Quoted in Kaldor, *Global Civil Society*, p. 75. As Kaldor notes, the same sorts of processes were taking place also in India, South Africa and elsewhere.

6 Adam Michnik, "Confessions of a Converted Dissident," Essay for the Erasmus Prize, 2001; http://www.eurozine.com/article/2001-12-28-michnik-en.html. In the West, too, the term "totalitarian," which had been discredited by its association with Cold War conservative ideologues, came back into use on the left, along with a greater sensitivity to issues of legality and human rights which had previously been seen as bourgeois liberal concerns.

7 Kumar, *1989*, p. 157.

8 "Civil society is in power," said the Czech Jiri Dienstbier, cited by Jensen and Miszlivetz (forthcoming).

9 This section is indebted to a very substantial paper presented by Jody Jensen and Ferenc Miszlivetz and to other contributions to the CiSoNet conference organized by Peter Wagner at the EUI, Florence, in November 2003 (see Peter Wagner (ed.), *The Languages of Civil Society* (Oxford: Berghahn), forthcoming).

10 *The Dynamics of the Breakthrough in Eastern Europe: The Polish Experience* (Berkeley, CA: University of California Press, 1991).

11 Dahrendorf, *Reflections on the Revolution in Europe* (London: Chatto, 1990), pp. 85; 92–3.

12 "Virtuous Circles: Antipodean Reflections on Power, Institutions and Civil Society," *East European Politics and Societies*, 11:1, Winter 1997, p. 64.

13 Manfred Hildermaier, Jürgen Kocka and Christoph Conrad (eds.), *Europäische Zivilgesellschaft in Ost und West: Begriffe, Geschichte, Chancen* (Frankfurt am Main: Campus, 2000), p. 8.

14 R. Fine and S. Rai (eds.) *Civil Society: Democratic Perspectives* (London: Cass, 1997).

15 G. Pollock, "Civil Society and Euro-Nationalism," *Studies in Social and Political Thought 4*, pp. 31–56, 2001; *Civil Society and Nation*, unpublished PhD thesis, University of Sussex, 2002.

16 Jensen and Miszlivetz refer to the "linguistic turn" in civil society discourse.

17 "The Public Sphere and a European Civil Society," in Jeff Alexander (ed.), *Real Civil Societies* (London: Sage, 1998), pp. 211–38.

18 L. Siedentop, *Democracy in Europe* (London: Allen Lane, 2000), p. 88.

19 Cf. Klaus Eder, "Zur Transformation nationalstaatlicher Öffentlichkeit in Europa," *Berliner Journal für Soziologie* 10: 2 (2000), pp. 167–84.

20 *Civil Society: Old Images, New Visions* (Cambridge: Polity, 1998).

21 This is stressed by Shin Jong-Hwa, Jean Terrier, and Peter Wagner in "The Languages of Civil Society: Varieties of Interpretation," in Peter Wagner (ed.), *The Languages of Civil Society.*

22 I addressed these issues in my "Steering the Public Sphere: Communication Policy in State Socialism and After," in Barbara Einhorn, Mary Kaldor and Zdenek Kavan (eds.), *Citizenship and Democratic Control in Contemporary Europe* (Cheltenham: Elgar, 1996), pp. 159–72. Some commentators would want to say that a public sphere which is only partly free is not a public sphere at all; I would take a more optimistic view of the possibility of relatively free discussion even in a fundamentally unfree context such as that of an authoritarian state. I myself participated occasionally in discussions of this kind in East Germany, both at universities and in discussion meetings organized by the Party's youth organization, the FDJ.

23 Habermas, *Between Facts and Norms* (Cambridge: Polity, 1992), p. 442.

24 See my contribution to Alan Sica and Stephen Turner (eds.), *The Disobedient Generation: 68ers and the Transformation of Social Theory* (Chicago: University of Chicago Press, 2005), pp. 281–302.

Chapter 8 Is There a European Society?

1 Martin Shaw, *Theory of the Global State* (Cambridge: Cambridge University Press, 2000), pp. 175–6.

2 There are also of course other European institutions, though I shall not examine them here.

3 The comparison is a little unfair, since the superpower was the USSR rather than just the Russian Federation, but the general point holds.

4 Either directly, in the form of EU membership or prospective membership, or in membership of the European Economic Area or, for the EU's "near abroad," participation in a wide variety of association agreements. However big a deal membership may be for new or prospective members, its importance for the Union as a whole diminishes as the Union itself expands. The old differentiation between a *Kleineuropa* grounded in the EC member-states and a broader *Grosseuropa* spanning the subcontinent is no longer particularly salient.

5 Renan, "Qu'est qu'une nation?," lecture of 1882, reprinted in his *Discours et conférences* (various translations). Renan's theme was picked up by the sociologist Marcel Mauss in two works published in 1920: "La nation" (*L'Année Sociologique*, pp. 7–68, and "La nation et l'internationalisme," delivered to a conference on "The Problem of Nationality" (*Proceedings of the Aristotelian Society* 20, 1920), pp. 242–51. Cf. Beck, *Das kosmopolitische Europa* (Frankfurt: Suhrkamp, 2004), pp. 17ff.

6   For an excellent summary and analysis of much of this historical writing, see Gurminder Bhambra, "Contesting Modernity" (unpublished PhD thesis, University of Sussex).

7   Stefan Aust and Michael Schmidt-Klingenberg (eds.), *Experiment Europa* (Stuttgart and Munich: Deutsche Verlags-Anstalt, 2003), p. 89. This uncertainty is also of course a problem for so-called national cultures. Cf. Walter Abish's novel, *How German Is It?* (New York: New Directions, 1983), and James Donald, "How English Is It?," in James Donald, *Sentimental Education: Schooling, Popular Culture, and the Regulation of Liberty* (London: Verso, 1992).

8   As Beck has noted in *Der kosmopolitischer Blick*, the contrast between Fukuyama and Huntington in many ways replays the Valladolid conference of 1550, between universalistic inclusionism (they too can become Christians) and particularistic rejection of the "savages" (Frankfurt: Suhrkamp, 2004), pp. 78–85.

9   Eugen Weber, *Peasants into Frenchmen: The Modernization of Rural France, 1870–1914* (Stanford, CA: Stanford University Press, 1979).

10   *Europe: Journey to an Unknown Destination* (Harmondsworth: Penguin, 1973).

11   Cf. Beck and Grande, *Das kosmopolitische Europa* (Frankfurt: Suhrkamp, 2004), Chapter III.

12   Cf. Beck and Grande, pp. 18ff.

13   Charlotte Girard, "Contracting and Founding in Times of Conflict," in Nathalie Karagiannis and Peter Wagner (eds.) *Ways of Worldmaking* (Liverpool University Press, forthcoming).

14   The Parliament's continuing peripatetic habit is just one of the factors reducing its credibility.

15   "Is There a Society Called Euro?," in Roland Axtmann (ed.), *Globalization and Europe* (London and New York: Continuum, 1998).

16   Ibid., p. 205.

17   "European Civil Society or Transnational Social Spaces," *European Journal of Social Theory*, 6: 1 (2003), pp. 36–7. For a different view, closer to my own though clearly somewhat rosy, see Beck and Grande, *Das kosmopolitische Europa*, p. 196. For them, "it is the political constructivism inherent in the concept of civil society which makes it so opportune and operative for the EU."

18   *Banal Nationalism* (London: Sage, 1995).

19   Weather forecasts are especially interesting. The old West German weather forecast used to cover the (rather larger) Germany with the frontiers of 1937; conversely, the UK national weather forecasts mostly ignore the contiguous territories of the Irish Republic and of north-western France.

20   Cf. Rumford, "European Civil Society," p. 30.

21   See, for example, Schlesinger and Kevin in *Democracy in the European Union* (London: Routledge, 2000, pp. 222–9), who also point to Euronews, launched

in 1993 on a transnational public service broadcasting base and transmitting in the major West European languages; this, however, is very uneven in its European reach.

22 Keith Middlemas, *Orchestrating Europe: The Informal Politics of the European Union, 1943–95* (London: Fontana, 1995), p. 685. See also Gerard Delanty and Chris Rumford, *Rethinking Europe, Social Theory and the Implications of Europeanization.* (London: Routledge, 2005).

23 Habermas (1976, p. 116).

24 Karl Deutsch et al., *International Political Communities* (New York: Anchor Books, 1966), p. 2.

25 In the days before writing these lines, for example, I listened to French radio news, bought a copy of *Le Monde* at the Sussex University newsagent (from, as it happened, a French student) and booked a train ticket to Paris on a website – all this against a background of more domestic listening, reading and travelling.

26 Jan Delhey, p. 20 "European Social Integration. From Convergence of Countries to Transnational Relations Between Peoples," Discussion Paper 201. (Berlin: WZB).

27 *Das kosmopolitische Europa*; see, in particular, Chapter 2, section 3, pp. 57–60.

28 *The Sources of Social Power*, 2 vols. (Cambridge: Cambridge University Press, 1986, 1993).

29 It is obvious, at least to this particular English-speaker, that the official language of the European Union ought to be English, just as it is obvious that its principal institutions should all be centralized in Brussels, but no-one quite dares to say so.

30 Colin Crouch, *Industrial Relations and European State Traditions* (Oxford: Clarendon Press 1993). See also Crouch, *Social Change in Western Europe* (Oxford: Oxford University Press, 1999).

31 "Europäische Identitätsbildung," in R. Viehoff and R.T. Segers, *Kultur, Identität, Europa* (Frankfurt: Suhrkamp, 1999), p. 249. Here Münch echoes Karl Deutsch who, with his focus on international relations, was relaxed about what he called a "layer-cake" pattern in which elites were relatively integrated and the passive masses less so. See K.W. Deutsch and W.J. Foltz, *Nation-Building* (London: Atherton, 1963).

32 Ulrich Beck and Edgar Grande, *Das kosmopolitische Europa* (Frankfurt: Suhrkamp, 2004), p. 196.

33 Ibid., pp. 230–1.

34 Habermas, "Europe's Second Chance," trans. in Habermas, *The Past as Future* (Cambridge: Polity, 1994). See also Habermas, *The Postnational Constitution* (Cambridge: Polity, 2001).

Bibliography

Abish, Walter (1980) *How German Is It?* (New York: New Directions).

Adler, Max (1922) "Die Staatsauffassung des Marxismus," in M.A. Hilferding and R. Hilferding (eds.), *Marx-Studien*, vol. IV (Vienna, reprinted Darmstadt: Wissenschaftliche Buchgesellschaft, 1973).

Adler, Max (1936) *Das Rätsel der Gesellschaft: Zur erkenntniskritischen Grundlegung der Sozialwissenschaft* (Vienna: Saturn-Verlag).

Adler, Max (1978) "The Relation of Marxism to Classical German Philosophy," in Tom Bottomore and Patrick Goode (eds.), *Austro-Marxism* (Oxford: Clarendon Press).

Adorno, Theodor (1956) *Dissonanzen*, 4th edn. (Göttingen: Vandenhoeck and Ruprecht, 1969).

Adorno, Theodor (1968) *Vorlesung zur Einleitung in die Soziologie* (Frankfurt: Junius, 1973).

Adorno, Theodor (1967–68) "Sociology and Psychology," *New Left Review* 46 (November–December 1967), pp. 67–80; 47 (January–February 1968), pp. 79–97.

Adorno, Theodor (1969) "A European Scholar in America," in D. Fleming and B. Bailyn (eds.), *The Intellectual Migration* (Cambridge, MA: Harvard University Press).

Adorno, Theodor (1972) *Gesammelte Schriften*, vol. 8 (Frankfurt: Suhrkamp).

Adorno, Theodor et al. (1969) *The Positivist Dispute in German Sociology* (London: Heinemann, 1976).

Albrow, Martin (1996) *The Global Age* (Cambridge: Polity).

Albrow, Martin and King, Elizabeth (eds.) (1990) *Globalization, Knowledge and Society* (London: Sage).

Anderson, Benedict (1983) *Imagined Communities: Reflections on the Origin and Spread of Nationalism* (London: New Left Books).

Archer, Margaret (1988) *Culture and Agency* (Cambridge: Cambridge University Press).

155

Bibliography

Archer, Margaret (1995) *Realist Social Theory: The Morphogenetic Approach* (Cambridge: Cambridge University Press).

Archer, Margaret (1996) "Social Integration and System Integration: Developing the Distinction," *Sociology* 30: 4, pp. 679–99.

Aust, Stefan and Schmidt-Klingenberg, Michael (eds.) (2003) *Experiment Europa* (Stuttgart: Deutsche Verlags-Anstalt).

Baczko, Bronislaw (1984) *Les imaginaires sociaux* (Paris: Payot).

Baker, Keith (1994) "Enlightenment and the Institution of Society: Notes for a Conceptual History," in W. Melching and W. Velema (eds.), *Main Trends in Cultural History* (Amsterdam: Rodopi).

Baker, Keith Michael (2001) "Enlightenment and the Institution of Society," in Sudipta Kaviraj and Sunil Khilnani (eds.), *Civil Society: History and Possibilities* (Cambridge: Cambridge University Press).

Barberis, Daniela (2003) "In Search of an Object: Organicist Sociology and the Reality of Society in *Fin-de-siècle* France," *History of the Human Sciences* 16: 3, pp. 51–72.

Baudrillard, Jean (1977) *Oublier Foucault* (Paris: Galilée).

Baudrillard, Jean (1978) *A l'ombre des majorités silencieuses: La fin du social* (Paris: Denoël-Gonthier, 1982); *In the Shadow of the Silent Majorities* (New York: Semiotext(e), 1983).

Baudrillard, Jean (1990) *Cool Memories* (London: Verso).

Bauman, Zygmunt (2002) *Society under Siege* (Cambridge: Polity).

Beck, Ulrich (1986) *The Risk Society: Towards a New Modernity* (London: Sage, 1992).

Beck, Ulrich (1987) "Beyond Class and Status," in Volker Meja, Dieter Misgeld and Nico Stehr (eds.), *Modern German Sociology* (New York: Columbia University Press).

Beck, Ulrich (2004) *Der kosmopolitischer Blick* (Frankfurt: Suhrkamp; trans. *The Cosmopolitan Vision* Cambridge: Polity, 2006).

Beck, Ulrich and Grande, Edgar (2004) *Das kosmopolitische Europa* (Frankfurt: Suhrkamp; trans. Cambridge: Polity, forthcoming).

Becker, Gary (1976) *The Economic Approach to Human Behavior* (Chicago: University of Chicago Press).

Becker, Gary (1996) *The Economics of Life* (New York: McGraw-Hill).

Bellah, Robert (1991) *The Good Society* (New York: Knopf).

Bellah, Robert et al. (1986) *Habits of the Heart: Individualism and Commitment in American Life* (Berkeley, CA: University of California Press).

Benton, Ted (2001) "Why are Sociologists Naturophobes?" in José López and Gary Potter (eds.), *After Postmodernism: An Introduction to Critical Realism* (London: Athlone), pp. 133–45.

Berger, Peter and Luckmann, Thomas (1966) *The Social Construction of Reality: An Essay in the Sociology of Knowledge* (Harmondsworth: Penguin).

Bibliography

Bhaskar, Roy (1975) *A Realist Theory of Science* (Leeds: Leeds Books).

Bhaskar, Roy (1979) *The Possibility of Naturalism* (Brighton: Harvester).

Billig, Michael (1995) *Banal Nationalism* (London: Sage).

Birnbaum, Pierre (1975) *La fin du politique* (Paris: Seuil).

Boltanski, Luc and Chiapello, Ève (1999) *Le nouvel esprit du capitalisme* (Paris: Gallimard).

Bottomore, Tom and Goode, Patrick (eds.) (1978) *Austro-Marxism* (Oxford: Clarendon Press).

Boudon, Raymond (1977) *Effets pervers et ordre social* (Paris: Presses Universitaires de France).

Bourdieu, Pierre (1974) *Outline of a Theory of Practice* (Cambridge: Cambridge University Press).

Brown, Phillip and Lauder, Hugh (2001) *Capitalism and Social Progress: The Future of Society in a Global Economy* (Basingstoke: Palgrave).

Buckley, Walter (1967) *Sociology and Modern Systems Theory* (Englewood Cliffs, NJ: Prentice-Hall).

Calhoun, Craig (1991) "Indirect Relationships and Imagined Communities: Large-Scale Social Integration and the Transformation of Everyday Life," in Pierre Bourdieu and James S. Coleman (eds.), *Social Theory for a Changing Society* (Boulder, CO: Westview Press).

Chakrabarty, Dipesh (2000) *Provincializing Europe: Postcolonial Thought and Historical Difference* (Princeton, NJ: Princeton University Press).

Chase-Dunn, Christopher (1989) *Global Formation: Structures of the World-Economy* (Oxford: Blackwell).

Chernilo, Daniel (2004) "Sociology and the Nation–State," unpublished PhD thesis, University of Warwick.

Chernilo, Daniel (forthcoming) "Social Theory's Methodological Nationalism: Myth and Reality," *European Journal of Social Theory*.

Clark, Jon and Diani, Marco (eds.) (1996) *Alain Touraine* (London: Falmer Press).

Clastres, Pierre (1974) *Society against the State* (trans. Oxford: Blackwell, 1977).

Cohen, Daniel (1999) *Nos temps modernes* (Paris: Flammarion).

Cohen, Jean (1983) *Class and Civil Society* (Oxford: Martin Robertson).

Cohen, Jean and Arato, Andrew (1992) *Civil Society and Political Theory* (Cambridge, MA: MIT Press).

Coleman, James (1990) *Foundations of Social Theory* (Cambridge, MA: Harvard University Press).

Coser, Lewis (1956) *The Functions of Social Conflict* (New York: Free Press).

Coser, Lewis (1965) *Georg Simmel* (Englewood Cliffs, NJ: Prentice-Hall).

Crothers, Charles (1996) *Social Structure* (London: Routledge).

Crouch, Colin (1993) *Industrial Relations and European State Traditions* (Oxford: Clarendon Press).

Bibliography

Dahrendorf, Ralf (1990) *Reflections on the Revolution in Europe* (London: Chatto).

Danermark, Berth et al. (2002) *Explaining Society* (London: Routledge).

Davis, Kingsley (1959) "The Myth of Functional Analysis as a Special Method in Sociology and Anthropology," *American Sociological Review* 24: 6 (December), pp. 757–72.

Delanty, Gerard (2000) *Modernity and Postmodernity* (Beverly Hills, CA: Sage).

Delanty, Gerard (2003) *Community* (London: Routledge).

Delanty, Gerard (2005) "Modernity and the Escape from Eurocentrism," in Gerard Delanty (ed.), *Handbook of Contemporary European Social Theory* (Beverly Hills, CA: Sage).

Delanty, Gerard and Rumford, Chris (2005) *Rethinking Europe, Social Theory and the Implications of Europeanization* (London: Routledge).

Deutsch, Karl et al. (1966) *International Political Communities* (New York: Anchor Books).

Donald, James (1992) "How English Is It?" in James Donald, *Sentimental Education: Schooling, Popular Culture, and the Regulation of Liberty* (London: Verso).

Donzelot, Jacques (1977) *The Policing of Families* (London: Hutchinson, 1980).

Donzelot, Jacques (1984) *L'invention du social* (Paris: Fayard).

Dubet, François and Martuccelli, Danilo (1998) *Dans quelle société vivons-nous?* (Paris: Seuil).

Durkheim, Emile (1893) *The Division of Labor in Society* (New York: Free Press; London: Macmillan, 1984).

Durkheim, Emile (1895) *The Rules of Sociological Method* (New York: Free Press; London: Macmillan, 1982).

Durkheim, Emile (1897a) *Suicide: A Sociological Study* (New York: Free Press; London: Routledge, 1963).

Durkheim, Emile (1897b) Review of Labriola, *Revue Philosophique* 44, pp. 645–51.

Durkheim, Emile (1899) "Note: Morphologie sociale," *L'Année Sociologique* 2, pp. 520–1.

Durkheim, Emile (1925) *L'Education morale* (Paris: Alcan).

Durkheim, Emile (1995) *The Elementary Forms of Religious Life* (London: Free Press).

Eder, Klaus (2000) "Zur Transformation nationaalstaatlicher Öffentlichkeit in Europa," *Berliner Journal für Soziologie* 10: 2, pp. 167–84.

Ehrenberg, Alain (1998) *La fatigue d'être soi* (Paris: Odile Jacob).

Eisenstadt, Shmuel (2003) *Comparative Civilizations and Multiple Modernities* (Leiden: Brill).

Elias, Norbert (1987) "The Retreat of Sociologists into the Present," *Theory, Culture & Society* 4: 2–3 (June), pp. 223–47.

Elias, Norbert (1991) *The Society of Individuals*, ed. Michael Schröter (Oxford: Blackwell).

158

Bibliography

Engels, Friedrich (1878) *Anti-Dühring* (*Marx-Engels-Werke*, vol. 20) (Berlin: Dietz, 1962).

Faye, Jean Pierre (1972) *Les langages totalitaires* (Paris: Hermann).

Fine, Robert and Rai, Shireen (eds.) (1997) *Civil Society: Democratic Perspectives* (London: Cass).

Foucault, Michel (1976) *Society Must Be Defended* (London: Allen Lane, 2003).

Frankfurt Institute for Social Research (1956) *Aspects of Sociology* (London: Heinemann, 1973).

Freitag, Michel (1986a) *Dialectique et société 1: Introduction à une théorie générale du Symbolique* (Montréal: Editions Saint-Martin).

Freitag, Michel (1986b) *Dialectique et société 2: Culture, pouvoir, contrôle: Les modes formels de reproduction de la société* (Montréal: Editions Saint-Martin).

Freitag, Michel (2002) *L'oubli de la société* (Rennes: Presses Universitaires de Rennes).

Freitag, Michel (2002) "The Dissolution of Society within the 'Social'," *European Journal of Social Theory* 5 (May), pp. 175–98.

Frisby, David (1984) *Georg Simmel* (revised edn., London: Routledge, 2002).

Frisby, David and Sayer, Derek (1986) *Society* (Chichester: Ellis Horwood).

Gane, Mike (1991) *Baudrillard: Critical and Fatal Theory* (London: Routledge).

Gane, Nicholas (2004) *The Future of Social Theory* (London: Continuum).

Gerhardt, Uta (1971) *Rollenanalyse als kritische Soziologie* (Neuwied: Luchterhand).

Giddens, Anthony (1972) "Four Myths in the History of Social Thought," *Economy and Society* 1, pp. 357ff. Reprinted in Anthony Giddens, *Studies in Social and Political Theory* (London: Hutchinson, 1977).

Giddens, Anthony (1984) *The Constitution of Society* (Cambridge: Polity).

Giddens, Anthony (1991) *Modernity and Self-Identity* (Cambridge: Polity).

Girard, Charlotte (2005) "Contracting and Founding in Times of Conflict," in Nathalie Karagiannis and Peter Wagner (eds.), *Ways of Worldmaking* (Liverpool: Liverpool University Press).

Granet, Marcel (1934) *La pensée chinoise* (Paris: La Renaissance du Livre).

Habermas, Jürgen (1991) "Europe's Second Chance," trans. in Jürgen Habermas, *The Past as Future* (Cambridge: Polity, 1994).

Habermas, Jürgen (1992) *Between Facts and Norms* (Cambridge: Polity, 1996).

Habermas, Jürgen (1998) *The Postnational Constitution* (Cambridge: Polity, 2001).

Habermas, Jürgen and Luhmann, Niklas (1971) *Theorie der Gesellschaft oder Sozialtechnologie?* (Frankfurt: Suhrkamp).

Hallberg, Peter and Wittrock, Björn (forthcoming) *The Return of Aristotle*, 2 vols.

Harré, Rom (1979) *Social Being* (Oxford: Blackwell),

Harré, Rom (1986) *Varieties of Realism* (Oxford: Blackwell).

Harré, Rom (1999) "Causal Mechanism and Social Practices," unpublished paper, November.

Bibliography

Harré, Rom (2002) "Social Reality and the Myth of Social Structure," *European Journal of Social Theory* 5: 1, pp. 111–23.

Hayek, Friedrich von (1955) *The Counter-Revolution in Science: Studies On the Abuse of Reason* (New York: Free Press).

Hegarty, Paul (2004) *Jean Baudrillard: Live Theory* (London: Continuum).

Hildermaier, Manfred, Kocka, Jürgen and Conrad, Christoph (eds.) (2000) *Europäische Zivilgesellschaft in Ost und West: Begriffe, Geschichte, Chancen* (Frankfurt: Campus).

Hirst, Paul Q. and Thompson, Grahame (1996) *Globalization in Question* (Cambridge: Polity).

Hobsbawm, Eric (1995) *The Age of Extremes: The Short Twentieth Century 1914–1991* (London: Abacus).

Hollis, Martin (1977) *Models of Man* (Cambridge: Cambridge University Press).

Hollis, Martin and Smith, Steve (1990) *Explaining and Understanding International Relations* (Oxford: Oxford University Press).

Holmwood, John (2005) "Functionalism and its Critics," in Austin Harrington (ed.), *Modern Social Theory: An Introduction* (Oxford: Oxford University Press), pp. 87–109.

Honneth, Axel (1992) *The Struggle for Recognition* (Cambridge: Polity, 1995).

Hopper, Paul (2005) *Rebuilding Communities in an Age of Individualism* (Aldershot: Ashgate).

Hume, David (1748) *An Enquiry Concerning Human Understanding*, ed. T.H. Green (London: A. Millar).

Institut für Sozialforschung (1956) *Soziologische Exkurse*, trans. as Institute for Social Research, *Aspects of Sociology* (London: Heinemann, 1973).

Jensen, Jody and Miszlivetz, Ferenc (2005) "The Languages of Civil Society – Europe and Beyond," in Peter Wagner (ed.), *The Languages of Civil Society* (Oxford: Berghahn).

Kaldor, Mary (2003) *Global Civil Society: An Answer to War* (Cambridge: Polity).

Karagiannis, Nathalie and Wagner, Peter (2005, forthcoming) "Rethinking the Social and the Political: Towards a Theory of Synagonism," *Journal of Political Philosophy*.

Kaviraj, Sudipta and Khilnani, Sunil (eds.) (2001) *Civil Society: History and Possibilities* (Cambridge: Cambridge University Press).

Keane, John (ed.) (1988) *Civil Society and the State: New European Perspectives* (London: Verso).

Keane, John (1998) *Civil Society: Old Images, New Visions* (Cambridge: Polity).

Kratochwil, Friedrich (2005) "Global Governance and the Emergence of 'World Society'" in Peter Wagner (ed.), *The Languages of Civil Society* (Oxford: Berghahn).

Kroker, Arthur and Crook, David (1988) *The Postmodern Scene: Excremental Culture and Hyper-Aesthetics* (Basingstoke: Macmillan Education).

Bibliography

Krygier, Martin (1997) "Virtuous Circles: Antipodean Reflections on Power, Institutions and Civil Society," *East European Politics and Societies* 11: 1 (winter), pp. 36–88.

Kumar, Krishan (2001) "Civil Society," in Krishan Kumar, *1989: Revolutionary Ideas and Ideals* (Minneapolis, MN: Minnesota University Press).

Latour, Bruno (1991) *We Have Never Been Modern* (trans. Cambridge: MA: Harvard University Press, 1993).

Latour, Bruno (2004) "The Social as Association," in Nicholas Gane (ed.), *The Future of Social Theory* (London: Continuum), pp. 77–90.

Latour, Bruno and Woolgar, Steve (1979) *Laboratory Life: The Social Construction of Scientific Facts* (London: Sage).

Lipovetsky, Gilles (1983) *L'ère du vide: Essais sur l'individualisme contemporain* (Paris: Gallimard).

Lockwood, David (1964) "Social Integration and System Integration," in G.K. Zollschan and W. Hirsch (eds.), *Explorations in Social Change* (London: Routledge).

López, José and Potter, Gary (eds.) (2001) *After Postmodernism: An Introduction to Critical Realism* (London: Athlone).

López, José and Scott, John (2000) *Social Structure* (Buckingham: Open University Press).

Ludz, Peter C. (1979) "Die Bedeutung der Soziologie für die politische Wissenschaft: Zur wissenschaftssoziologischen Interpretation des Streites um die politische Soziologie in den fünfziger Jahren," in G. Lüschen (ed.), *Deutsche Soziologie seit 1945, Kölner Zeitschrift für Soziologie und Sozialpsychologie, Sonderheft* 21, (Opladen: Westdeutscher Verlag), pp. 264–93.

Luhmann, Niklas (1997a) *Die Gesellschaft der Gesellschaft* (Frankfurt: Suhrkamp).

Luhmann, Niklas (1997b) "Globalization or World Society: How to Conceive of Modern Society," *International Review of Sociology* 7: 1 (March), pp. 67–80.

Lukács, Georg (1923) *History and Class Consciousness* (trans. London: Merlin Press, 1971).

Lukes, Steven (1970) "Methodological individualism reconsidered," in D. Emmett and A. MacIntyre (eds.), *Sociological Theory and Philosophical Analysis* (London: Macmillan).

Lukes, Steven (1973) *Individualism* (Oxford: Blackwell).

Lyotard, Jean-François (1979) *La condition postmoderne: Rapport sur le savoir* (Paris: Minuit; trans. Geoff Bennington and Brian Massumi as *The Postmodern Condition: A Report on Knowledge*, Minneapolis, MN: University of Minnesota Press, 1984).

Lyotard, Jean-François (1986) *Le postmoderne expliqué aux enfants* (Paris: Gallilée; trans. as *The Post Modern Explained to Children*, London: Turnaround, 1992).

MacIntyre, Alasdair (1979) *After Virtue* (London: Duckworth).

McLuhan, Marshall (1962) *The Gutenberg Galaxy* (London: Routledge).

161

Bibliography

Maffesoli, Michel (1982) *The Shadow of Dionysus* (Paris: Méridiens; Albany: SUNY Press, 1993).

Maffesoli, Michel (1985) *La connaissance ordinaire: Précis de sociologie compréhensive* (Paris: Méridiens; trans. as *Ordinary Knowledge*, Cambridge: Polity, 1996).

Maffesoli, Michel (1988) *The Times of the Tribes* (Paris: Méridiens).

Mann, Michael (1986, 1993) *The Sources of Social Power*, 2 vols. (Cambridge: Cambridge University Press).

Mann, Michael (1998) "Is there a Society Called Euro?" in Roland Axtmann (ed.), *Globalization and Europe* (London: Continuum), pp. 184–207.

Mannheim, Karl (1939) "The Concept of the State as an Organism," in Karl Mannheim, *Essays on Sociology and Social Psychology* (London: Routledge, 1953).

Margolis, J. (1989) "Postscript on Modernism and Postmodernism, Both," *Theory, Culture & Society* 6: 1, pp. 5–30.

Marshall, H.E. (1905) *Our Island Story: A History of England for Boys and Girls*, with pictures by A.S. Forrest (London: T.C. & E.C. Jack).

Marx, Karl (1894) *Capital*, vol. 3 (Harmondsworth: Penguin, 1976).

Marx, Karl (1973) *Grundrisse: Foundations of the Critique of Political Economy (Rough Draft)* (Harmondsworth: Penguin).

Marx, Karl and Engels, Friedrich (1848) *Manifesto of the Communist Party* (Harmondsworth: Penguin, 1967).

Mauss, Marcel (1920a) "La nation," *L'Année Sociologique* 3 (1953–54), pp. 7–68.

Mauss, Marcel (1920b) "La nation et l'internationalisme," *Proceedings of the Aristotelian Society* 20, pp. 242–51.

Mestrovic, Stepan (1993) *Émile Durkheim and the Reformulation of Sociology* (Lanham, MD: Rowman and Littlefield).

Michels, Robert (1911) *Political Parties: A Sociological Study of the Oligarchical Tendencies of Modern Democracy* (New York: Free Press, 1962).

Michnik, Adam (2001) "Confessions of a Converted Dissident," essay for the Erasmus Prize, http://www.eurozine.com/article/2001-12-28-michnik-en.html

Middlemas, Keith (1995) *Orchestrating Europe: The Informal Politics of the European Union, 1943–95* (London: HarperCollins).

Mitzman, Arthur (1973) *Sociology and Estrangement: Three Sociologists of Imperial Germany* (New York: Knopf).

Mommsen, Wolfgang (1974) *The Age of Bureaucracy* (Oxford: Blackwell).

Montesquieu, Baron de (1748) *L'esprit des lois* (Paris: Edition-Touquet, 1821).

Moore, Barrington (1972) *Injustice: Reflections on the Causes of Human Misery* (London: Allen Lane).

Moore, W.E. (1978) "Functionalism," in Tom Bottomore and Robert Nisbet (eds.), *A History of Sociological Analysis* (New York: Basic Books).

Müller-Doohm, Stefan (2003) *Adorno: Eine Biographie* (Frankfurt: Suhrkamp). Tr. Cambridge: Polity, 2005.

Bibliography

Münch, Richard (1999) "Europäische Identitätsbildung," in R. Viehoff and R.T. Segers, *Kultur, Identität, Europa* (Frankfurt: Suhrkamp).

Nancy, Jean-Luc (1986) *The Inoperative Community* (trans. Minneapolis, MN: University of Minnesota Press, 1991).

Neocleous, Mark (2003) *Imagining the State* (Maidenhead: Open University Press).

Nicholson, Linda and Seidman, Steve (eds.) (1995) *Social Postmodernism: Beyond Identity Politics* (Cambridge: Cambridge University Press).

Nisbet, Robert (1966) *The Sociological Tradition* (New York: Basic Books).

Offe, Claus (1985) *Disorganized Capitalism* (Cambridge: Polity).

Olsen, Mancur (1965) *The Logic of Collective Action* (Cambridge, MA: Harvard University Press).

O'Neill, John (1972) *Sociology as a Skin Trade* (London: Heinemann).

Osborne, Peter (1995) *The Politics of Time: Modernity and Avant-Garde* (London: Verso).

Outhwaite, William (1979) "Social Thought and Social Science," in *New Cambridge Modern History*, vol. XIII (Companion Volume) (Cambridge: Cambridge University Press 1979), pp. 271–92.

Outhwaite, William (1983) *Concept Formation in Social Science* (London: Routledge).

Outhwaite, William (1987) *New Philosophies of Social Science* (London: Macmillan).

Outhwaite, William (1995) "Nietzsche and Critical Theory," in Peter Sedgwick (ed.), *Nietzsche: A Critical Reader* (Oxford: Blackwell).

Outhwaite, William (1996a) "Social Action and the Production of Society," in Jon Clark and Marco Diani (eds.), *Alain Touraine* (London: Falmer Press).

Outhwaite, William (1996b) "Steering the Public Sphere: Communication Policy in State Socialism and After," in Barbara Einhorn, Mary Kaldor and Zdenek Kavan (eds.), *Citizenship and Democratic Control in Contemporary Europe* (Cheltenham: Elgar), pp. 159–72.

Outhwaite, William (1998) "Naturalisms and Antinaturalisms," in Tim May and Malcolm Williamson (eds.), *Knowing the Social World* (Milton Keynes: Open University Press), pp. 22–36.

Outhwaite, William (1999) "The Myth of Modernist Method," *European Journal of Social Theory* 2 (February), pp. 5–25.

Outhwaite, William (2001) "What is European Culture?" in W. Ehlert and G. Széll (eds.), *New Democracies and Old Societies in Europe* (Frankfurt: Peter Lang), pp. 92–101.

Outhwaite, William (2004) "Intentional and Reflexive Objectivity: Some Reflections," in Margaret Archer and William Outhwaite (eds.), *Defending Objectivity: Essays in Honour of Andrew Collier* (London: Routledge), pp. 226–36.

Outhwaite, William (2005a) "Hermeneutic and Phenomenological Approaches," in Mark Risjord and Stephen Turner (eds.), *Handbook of the Philosophy of Sociology and Anthropology* (Oxford: Elsevier).

Bibliography

Outhwaite, William (2005b) "European Transformations," in Gerard Delanty (ed.), *Handbook of Contemporary European Social Theory* (London: Sage).

Outhwaite, William (2005c) "From Switzerland to Sussex," in Alan Sica and Stephen Turner (eds.), *The Disobedient Generation: 68ers and the Transformation of Social Theory* (Chicago: University of Chicago Press), pp. 281–302.

Outhwaite, William and Ray, Larry (2005) *Social Theory and Postcommunism* (Oxford: Blackwell).

Paine, Thomas (1976) *Common Sense*, ed. I. Kramnick (Harmondsworth: Penguin).

Parsons, Talcott (1968) *The Structure of Social Action* (New York: Free Press), pp. 89–94.

Pérez-Días, Victor (1998) "The Public Sphere and a European Civil Society," in Jeff Alexander (ed.), *Real Civil Societies* (London: Sage), pp. 211–38.

Pickering, W.S.F. (2000) *Durkheim and Representations* (London: Routledge).

Pollock, G. (2001) "Civil Society and Euro-Nationalism," *Studies in Social and Political Thought* 4, pp. 31–56.

Pollock, G. (2002) "Civil Society and Nation," unpublished PhD thesis, University of Sussex.

Popper, Karl (1957) *The Poverty of Historicism* (London: Routledge and Kegan Paul).

Radcliffe-Brown, A.R. (1952) *Structure and Function in Primitve Society: Essays and Addresses* (London: Cohen and West).

Rattansi, Ali (1995) "Just Framing: Ethnicities and Racisms in a 'Postmodern' Framework," in Linda Nicholson and Steve Seidman (eds.), *Social Postmodernism: Beyond Identity Politics* (Cambridge: Cambridge University Press), pp. 250–86.

Renan, Ernest (1982) "Qu'est qu'une nation?" reprinted in Ernest Renan, *Discours et conférences* (vol. 5 of *Œuvres complètes*), ed. H. Psichari (Paris: Calmann-Levy, 1947; various translations).

Rojek, Chris and Turner, Bryan (1993) *Forget Baudrillard* (London: Routledge).

Rose, Nikolas (1996) " 'The Death of the Social'? Re-figuring the Territory of Government," *Economy and Society* 25: 3, pp. 327–56.

Rosenau, P.M. (1992) *Post-Modernism and the Social Sciences* (Princeton, NJ: Princeton University Press).

Rosenberg, Justin (2000) *The Follies of Globalisation Theory* (London: Verso).

Rousseau, J.-J. (1754) "A Discourse on the Origin of Inequality among Men," in J.-J. Rousseau, *The Social Contract and the Discourses*, trans. G.D.H. Cole (London: Dent, 1913).

Rumford, Chris (2003) "European Civil Society or Transnational Social Spaces," *European Journal of Social Theory* 6: 1, pp. 36–7.

Runciman, W.G. (ed.) (1978) *Max Weber: Selections in Translation* (Cambridge: Cambridge University Press),

Sandel, Michael (1982) *Liberalism and the Limits of Justice* (Cambridge: Cambridge University Press).

164

Bibliography

Sayer, Andrew (2000) *Realism and Social Science* (London: Sage).

Schlesinger, Philip and Kevin, Deirder (2000) "Can the European Union Become a Sphere of Politics?" in Erik Oddvar Eriksen and John Erik Fossum (eds.), *Democracy in the European Union: Integration Through Deliberation?* (London: Routledge), pp. 206–29.

Schmidt, Alfred (1968) *The Concept of Nature in Marx* (London: New Left Books, 1971).

Schmidt, Alfred (1969) *Beiträge zur marxistischen Erkenntnistheorie* (Frankfurt: Suhrkamp).

Schrader-Klebert, Karin (1968) "Der Begriff der Gesellschaft als regulative Idee: Zur transzendentalen Begründung der Soziologie bei Georg Simmel," *Soziale Welt* 19: 2, pp. 97–118.

Schutz, Alfred (1932) *The Phenomenology of the Social World* (London: Heinemann, 1972).

Schwinn, Thomas (2001) *Differenzierung ohne Gesellschaft* (Weilerswist: Velbrück).

Sedgwick, Peter (ed.) (1995) *Nietzsche: A Critical Reader* (Oxford: Blackwell).

Sennett, Richard (1998) *Corrosion of Character: The Personal Consequences of Work in the New Capitalism* (New York: W.W. Norton).

Shaw, Martin (2000) *Theory of the Global State* (Cambridge: Cambridge University Press).

Shin Jong-Hwa, Terrier, Jean and Wagner, Peter (2005) "Varieties of Interpretation," in Peter Wagner (ed.), *The Languages of Civil Society* (Oxford: Berghahn).

Shonfield, Andrew (1973) *Europe: Journey to an Unknown Destination* (Harmondsworth: Penguin).

Shore, Cris (2003) "Community," in William Outhwaite (ed.), *The Blackwell Dictionary of Modern Social Thought* (Oxford: Blackwell), pp. 101–2.

Siedentop, Larry (2000) *Democracy in Europe* (London: Allen Lane).

Silver, H. and Wilkinson, F. (1995) "Policies to Combat Social Exclusion: A French–British Comparison," in G. Rogers et al., *Social Exclusion* (Geneva: International Institute for Labour Studies).

Simmel, Georg (1890) *Über soziale Differenzierung* (Leipzig: Duncker und Humblot).

Simmel, Georg (1892) *The Problems of the Philosophy of History* (New York: Free Press, 1977).

Simmel, Georg (1892–93) *Einleitung in die Moralwissenschaft* (Berlin: Hertz).

Simmel, Georg (1908) "How is Society Possible?" in Georg Simmel, *Soziologie* (Leipzig: Duncker und Humblot); trans. in K. Wolff (ed.), *Georg Simmel* (Columbus, OH: Ohio State University Press, 1959).

Simmel, Georg (1912) "The Concept and Tragedy of Culture," in Georg Simmel, *The Conflict in Modern Culture and Other Essays* (New York: Teachers College Press, 1968), pp. 27–46.

165

Bibliography

Simmel, Georg (1931) *Soziologische Vorlesungen von Georg Simmel*, ed. Society for Social Research, University of Chicago.

Solms-Laubach, Franz (2005) *Nietzsche and Early German and Austrian Sociology* (Berlin and New York: De Gruyter).

Sombart, Werner (1906) *Why Is There No Socialism in the United States?* (London: Macmillan, 1976).

Spencer, Herbert (1893) *The Principles of Sociology* (London: Williams and Norgate).

Staniszkis, Jadwiga (1991) *The Dynamics of the Breakthrough in Eastern Europe: The Polish Experience* (Berkeley, CA: University of California Press).

Stauth, G. and Turner, B.S. (1988) *Nietzsche's Dance: Resentment, Reciprocity and Distance in Social Life* (Oxford: Blackwell).

Stedman Jones, Sue (2000) "Representation in Durkheim's Masters: Kant and Renouvier," in W.S.F. Pickering, *Durkheim and Representations* (London: Routledge).

Stichweh, Rudolf (1994) "Differenz und Integration in der Weltgesellschaft," reprinted in Rudolf Stichweh, *Die Weltgesellschaft* (Frankfurt: Suhrkamp, 2000).

Stones, Rob (1996) *Sociological Reasoning: Towards a Past-Modern Sociology* (Basingstoke: Macmillan).

Taylor, Charles (1989) *Sources of the Self* (Cambridge, MA: Harvard University Press).

Taylor, Charles (2004) *Modern Social Imaginaries* (Durham, NC: Duke University Press).

Thatcher, Margaret (1987) Speech to Women's Institute (text available on various web locations).

Therborn, Göran (2004) *Between Sex and Power: Family in the World 1900–2000* (London: Routledge).

Tönnies, Ferdinand (1897) *Der Nietzsche-Kultus: Eine Kritik* (Leipzig: O.R. Reisland).

Tönnies, Ferdinand (1971) "My Relation to Sociology," in Ferdinand Tönnies, *On Sociology: Pure, Applied and Emiprical* (Chicago: University of Chicago Press).

Touraine, Alain (1954) "Le traitement de la société globale dans la sociologie américaine contemporaine," *Cahiers Internationaux de Sociologie* 16, pp. 126–45.

Touraine, Alain (1965) *Sociologie de l'action* (Paris: Seuil).

Touraine, Alain (1977) *La Société invisible* (Paris: Seuil).

Touraine, Alain (1980) "L'inutile idée de société," in R. Maggiori and C. Delacampagne (eds.), *Philosopher* (Paris: Fayard), pp. 237–45.

Touraine, Alain (1981) "Une sociologie sans société," *Revue Française de Sociologie* XXII, pp. 3–13.

Touraine, Alain (1984) *Le retour de l'acteur* (Paris: Seuil).

Touraine, Alain (1989) "Is Sociology Still the Study of Society?" *Thesis Eleven* 23, pp. 5–34.

Touraine, Alain (1992) *Critique of Modernity* (Oxford: Blackwell, 1995).

Touraine, Alain (1997) *Can We Live Together?* (Cambridge: Polity, 2000).

Bibliography

Touraine, Alain (1998) "Culture Without Society," *Cultural Values* 2: 1, pp. 140–57.

Touraine, Alain (1999) *Beyond Neoliberalism* (Cambridge: Polity, 2001).

Touraine, Alain (2001) "From Understanding Society to Discovering the Subject," paper delivered at the University of Sussex.

Touraine, Alain (2003) "Sociology Without Societies," *Current Sociology* 51: 2, pp. 123–32.

Urry, John (2000) *Sociology beyond Societies* (London: Routledge).

Vaihinger, Hans (1911) *The Philosophy of As-If* (trans. C.K. Ogden, London: Kegan Paul, 1924).

Veyne, Paul (1988) *Did the Greeks Believe in Their Myths?* (Chicago: University of Chicago Press).

Viroli, Maurizio (1990) "Machiavelli and the Republican Idea of Politics," in Gisela Bock, Quentin Skinner and Maurizio Viroli (eds.), *Machiavelli and Republicanism* (Cambridge: Cambridge University Press).

Wagner, Peter (1994) *A Sociology of Modernity: Liberty and Discipline* (London: Routledge).

Wagner, Peter (2001) *A History and Theory of the Social Sciences* (London: Sage).

Wallerstein, Immanuel (1974) *The Modern World System* (New York: Academic Press).

Wallerstein, Immanuel (1985) *Le Capitalisme historique*, 2nd edn. (Paris: La Découverte).

Wallerstein, Immanuel (1986) "Societal Development, or Development of the World-System?" reprinted in M. Albrow and E. King (eds.), *Globalization, Knowledge and Society* (London: Sage, 1990), pp. 157–71.

Walzer, Michael (1983) *Spheres of Justice* (Oxford: Martin Robertson).

Wang Hui (2005, forthcoming) "Imagining Asia: A Genealogical Analysis," previewed in *Le monde diplomatique*, February, pp. 20–2.

Weber, Eugen (1979) *Peasants into Frenchmen: The Modernization of Rural France, 1870–1914* (Stanford, CA: Stanford University Press).

Weber, Max (1903–6) *Roscher and Knies* (New York: Free Press, 1975).

Weber, Max (1904–5) *The Protestant Ethic and the "Spirit" of Capitalism* (trans. Stephen Kalberg, Los Angeles: Roxbury, 2001).

Weber, Max (1920) *Economy and Society*, 3 vols. (New York: Bedminster Press, 1968).

Weber, Max (1920–21) *The Sociology of Religion* (London: Methuen, 1966).

Weiss, Linda (1998) *The Myth of the Powerless State: Governing the Economy in a Global Era* (Cambridge: Polity).

Wolff, Kurt (ed.) (1950) *The Sociology of Georg Simmel* (Chicago: Free Press).

Wolff, Kurt (ed.) (1959) *Georg Simmel* (Columbus, OH: Ohio State University Press).

Wolin, Sheldon (1960) *Politics and Vision* (Boston: Little, Brown).

Zijderveld, Anton (1972) *The Abstract Society* (London: Allen Lane).

Index

critique of 4, 10
  global 45, 91
  origins of 58
Cardoso, F. 100
Castoriadis, C. 61
charisma 136
Charlemagne 111
Chase-Dunn, C. 141n
Chernilo, D. 77, 140n, 146n
citizen 11, 27, 101, 105, 124
citizenship 63, 113–14, 131
civil society 2, 12, 36, 69, 96–107,
    115–16, 118–20, 122–6, 152n
  European 116, 120, 122
  global 105
class 4, 9–11, 21, 23, 58, 61, 70–185,
    91, 100, 103, 129, 149
class conflict, struggle 9, 11, 60, 85
class consciousness 149
class structure 25
Clastres, P. 73, 125, 145n
Clinton, W. 31, 124
Cohen, D. 39–40, 138n
Cohen, J. 99, 105, 150n
Cold War 50, 113, 151n
Cole, G.D.H. 105
Coleman, J. 19
collective consciousness 6, 66
collectivism 2, 90, 136n
Collier, A. 144n
Collins, R.
common currency (*see also* Euro)
    117
common sense 14, 20, 42
communicative action etc. 64, 119,
    141n
communism 12, 73, 100, 104, 112,
    140n (*see also* state socialism)
Communist Manifesto 9, 57, 131n,
    139n, 140n
communitarian, -ism 28, 30–3,
    124

community ix, 1, 2, 4, 7, 8, 12, 13,
    17, 29–33, 58, 71, 93, 99, 109,
    119, 131n, 136n
  imagined 117
  of interest 116
  national 29, 40, 120
  political 114, 126
complexity 79, 94
Comte, A. 4, 5
constitution(alism) 101, 112, 115, 151
constitutional patriotism 120
crisis 114
critical theory (*see* Frankfurt School)
Crusoe, R. 23, 33
culture 1, 22, 47, 49, 50, 60, 62–3,
    67, 69, 80, 93, 95, 121
  European 38, 143n
  managerial 145n
  minister of 73
  national 116, 153n
  and society, social structure 90, 94
  tragedy of 7, 63
culture shock 112

Dahrendorf, R. 101–2, 132n, 151n
De Gaulle, C. 89
deconstruction 41, 43, 67, 135n, 138n
Delhey, J. 119, 154n
democracy vii, 30, 57, 63–4, 101,
    105, 113–14, 125
  associational 105
  Christian 12, 18
  cosmopolitan 131n
  people's democracies 100, 123
  radical 11, 131n
  social 11, 18, 21, 112
democratic deficit 115
Derrida, J. 110
differentiation 26, 51
division of labour 5–6
domination 63, 71, 111
Donzelot, J. 11, 92